AN INSPIRATIONAL BOOK FOR THE YOUTH

SANDY BURRELL

Copyright © 2022 Sandy Burrell

All rights reserved. No part of this book may be reproduced, stored, or transmitted by any means—whether auditory, graphic, mechanical, or electronic—without written permission of both publisher and author, except in the case of brief excerpts used in critical articles and reviews. Unauthorized reproduction of any part of this work is illegal and is punishable by law.

Scripture quotations taken from the New Revised Standard Version (NRSV). Copyright © 1989 the Division of Christian Education of the National Council of the Churches of Christ in the United States of America.

The Holy Bible, New International Version (NIV). Copyright © 1973, 1978, 1984, 2011 by Biblica, Inc.™. Used by permission. All rights reserved. www.xulonpress.com

ISBN: 979-8-88640-070-0 (sc)
ISBN: 979-8-88640-071-7 (hc)
ISBN: 979-8-88640-072-4 (e)

Because of the dynamic nature of the Internet, any web addresses or links contained in this book may have changed since publication and may no longer be valid. The views expressed in this work are solely those of the author and do not necessarily reflect the views of the publisher, and the publisher hereby disclaims any responsibility for them.

THE EWINGS PUBLISHING

One Galleria Blvd., Suite 1900, Metairie, LA 70001
1-888-421-2397

CONTENTS

Introduction v

Dedication ix

Chapter 1 Calling 1

Chapter 2 Words have Power 23

Chapter 3 Play to Your Own Strengths 43

Chapter 4 Influences and Inspirations 72

Chapter 5 Crisis Mode 103

Chapter 6 To the Future 127

Chapter 7 Message to the Parents 144

INTRODUCTION

"When I was a child, I spoke as a child, I thought like a child, I reasoned like a child; when I became an adult, I put an end to childish ways" (1 Cor. 13:11).

What's the appropriate age for something? That's always debatable. There is an ideal age. But that is not always the right time. Sound judgment will determine when the right time is. Decisions as always are 50-50 chance of win or lose. Stick to your guns no matter what and learn from the experience.

Youth are the future without question. But how are we preparing the future? Are we taking steps to make sure they are ready? Are we throwing them into a situation and hoping they figure it out without some sort of strategy? If we are teaching, do we over preach? Under preach? Or balance it out giving them enough to work with?

How do we share out knowledge and values? Do we ram it down their throats telling them it's this way or else? Do we sit back and hope they appreciate it? Or do we balance it out showing why something means a big deal to you? The more you talk about things in past tense the more it stays that way. We don't need to get "hip" with the message. But we do need to show how someone now, benefits from something that happened years ago.

Time spent the right way will yield good results. "Parable of the Sower" which ever version you read (Matt. 13:1-9, 18-23, Mk. 4:1-8, 14-20, or Lk. 8:4-8, 11-15) teaches that. All versions of that story mention that seed was scattered in three areas. And all said that it was when 'seeds fell on good soil' that yielded the best results with varying amounts.

If my Great Grandfather Sandy was still with us he would probably have a few things to say about planting and growing food given he was a farmer. When I used to visit my dad during breaks from school, I would ask how he planted his garden. He would say that the soil had to be prepared a certain way to yield results.

There are many ways to look at that biblical story. But I'm going to focus on the planting and growing part. You can't just plant seeds anywhere and expect results to happen. Environment among other conditions play a part in whether something will happen.

In our case, circumstances and environment among other factors play a part. Good or bad, events effect what happens. If you want to yield great results we have to do what we can to produce them. Of all the tools we have at our disposal "time" is the most important one of all. If it isn't used the right way it is wasted.

So the question is how are we using our time to build future leadership? How much is devoted to teaching, nurturing, developing, encouraging, let alone supporting potential leaders? If we don't have the resources what are we doing to find them?

This is where teachers and mentors become assets. Support and assistance for them is crucial. Training is a group effort. We either are successful as a group or a failure. As a group we can all pitch in on some level to make sure the next generation is ready. Then when the time comes we can confidently pass the torch to the next group and say it is your show now.

My former mentor who ran the Acolytes at my church has been urging me for awhile to write an inspirational book for the youth. My reservations were initially big because I doubted being able to do it. However reflecting on what went on when I grew up the idea became more specific. The title "Seed Time" is borrowed from a workshop I attended during my days with the National Society of Black Engineers. The focus of that workshop was about planting the seeds for the future. My predecessors who ran the Acolytes were about building leaders. And I am a product of that tutelage in the Acolytes.

When I was installed as Verger of my church a feeling of irony surfaced. My progression through the Acolytes becoming one of the group leaders, to the National Society of Black Engineers becoming Chapter President, to returning to the Acolytes becoming the head of the group ultimately being picked to become Verger, I never saw any leadership books from anyone but me. Following becoming Verger that is when I was presented with plenty of books to help me develop as a leader. Growth can happen at any point in time but when you are trying to figure out where you are going books like that could have come sooner.

The focus of the majority of the chapters here is to spark ideas that will help you grow and develop how to work within a group setting. As well as figure out how to develop who you are as a person let alone a leader. Even if you don't aspire to become a leader this book will help you develop to an extent critical thinking skills. Also growing up may come with some level of angst. So along with chapters that help develop who you are trying to be as a person there is a chapter that discusses how to react when bad things happen in life.

The book at times uses stories from the bible that fit the conversation. However I am not a minister or a member of the clergy. There is no expounding of theology here. At times you will see me borrow from events of what I experienced as a person that fits the discussion. In general my hope is this book will find an audience with the youth and anyone that is looking to grow as an individual. Also to create dialog with parents and children, there is only so much I can do. It isn't up to me to raise another person's child. That is still up to the parent. So the final chapter of this book is my passing the torch back to the parent. Before concluding I would like to thank Mr. Cecil Brewster for planting the seed for me to have an idea on writing this book. And I would also like to thank Ms. Ebony Rivers for encouraging me to keep on when I got discouraged writing this book her assistance at times was priceless.

DEDICATION

This work commemorates over 25 years of service in the Ministry of Acolytes (1987-present). The book is written in Thanksgiving to God for all of those who at some point during my journey had input into my growth as an individual. This includes the leaders of the following groups: Boy Scouts (Pack/ Troop 808) at Trinity Baptist Church, the Acolytes of St. Luke's Episcopal Church, the National Society of Black Engineers (New York Institute of Technology- Manhattan Chapter), and the Vergers Guild of the Episcopal Church.

CHAPTER ONE

"Consider your own call, brothers and sisters: not many of you were wise by human standards, not many were powerful, not many were of noble birth. But God chose what is foolish in the world to shame the wise; God chose what is weak in the world to shame the strong; God chose the low and despised in the world, things that are not, to reduce to nothing things that are, so that no one might boast in the presence of God" (1 Cor. 1:26-29).

My protégé once asked me about calling. Calling isn't convenient. It can happen at any time and any place. At some point I mentioned that talent and skill is good. However if you plan on being involved in something for the long haul, you need also reason and desire. Otherwise whatever you do will become a fad and forgettable.

When talking about calling not always being convenient. Consider the situations surrounding some of the figures that appear in the bible. When Moses was called he is tending a flock in the wilderness (Ex. 3:1). When Gideon was called by God he is beating wheat in a wine press

(Judg. 6:11). When Samuel comes to anoint David as king, David is initially off tending the sheep (1 Sam. 16:11). When Elijah comes to pick Elisha as his successor, Elisha is in the middle of plowing the field (1 Kings 19:19). Jesus called some of his early disciples while they were fishing (Matt. 4:18-22). When the Apostle Paul receives the call he was persecuting the church (Acts 9:1-9). In this handful of instances no one is really looking to be a leader on any level. But they gradually accept the call when given.

We are all called on to aid in some capacity or another and this might lead to a leadership position. However the way we respond to calling will determine the outcome. You are in the situation for a reason. And you are accountable for your actions and yours alone. Others may have had a hand in directing you into the situation but it is up to you what the outcome ultimately becomes.

You may not set out to become a leader. But whether you are associated with a group or on your own you make decisions. So to some extent you are a leader. With that said embrace the fact and move on. How effective and successful you are in a situation depends on you.

After careful examining of your calling, it is important to plan out how to approach the task set before you. So the idea of flying blind is not advised in this situation. To set goals you need to figure out what is possibly ahead for you to deal with. *"Desire without knowledge is not good, and one who moves too hurriedly misses the way"* (Prov. 19:2). Good sound advice goes a long way in this situation. Take a moment and think about it.

Before you go start an, "I am not worthy" chant. Take a moment and evaluate the situation. Is your calling an honest one, or is someone forcing his or her ambitions on you? Only you know for sure what is going on. I personally hope it is an honest one. Whichever the case may be there are ways to make things work in your favor. You can turn a negative into a positive one. If it is an honest one then that means someone sees you have a talent for something. And clearly doesn't want you to waste it. With that said try and eliminate all possible excuses for not answering the call.

Anything you do in life is a journey. You don't always have the skills, tools, resources, and so on for the job. So take an honest look at where and who you are as a person. Set realistic goals for yourself to achieve, while gathering the necessary tools to compensate for where you are lacking. With work you will get there. Just maintain patience and follow through. With that said let's eliminate some excuses:

You can easily say you are <u>too young</u>. *"Let no one despise your youth, but set the believers an example in speech and conduct, in love, in faith, in purity"* (1 Tim. 4:12). But no one is too young to answer the call when the time calls for leadership. If you are able to understand the concept of respect, you can learn how to be a good leader. Leaders are not born they are made. As a youth you learn how to read and write as well as how to speak among other skills. So in the process of learning these skills learn how to utilize them to work better with others. Good mentors will help you in this process. Also when you learn how to carry yourself in a respectful way towards others you will be able to overcome obstacles such as age gaps. To get respect you have to earn it. So when you set a positive example people will go to bat for you. It may not be right away but patience and time will work things out for you.

The Stanley Cup Finals in 2009 and 2010 saw the two youngest captains in league history lead their teams to championships. In 2009 Sidney Crosby captain of the Pittsburgh Penguins led his team to become Stanley Cup Champions in 2009. It was a measure of revenge for his team. Because they were defeated in the finals a year ago to the Detroit Red Wings and worst of all losing on home ice. The Penguins returned the favor by beating the Red Wings in Detroit.

Sidney Crosby was dubbed "The Next One". In only his second season (2006-2007) he led the league in scoring taking home the Art Ross Trophy, becoming the youngest player to do so and the only teenager. That same season he took home the Hart Trophy as the league MVP. Early in his career Sidney Crosby was considered a whiner and immature. Then again people complained that Wayne Gretzky was a whiner. But as time went on his reputation improved and he became one of the more iconic figures in hockey. In time maybe Sidney Crosby will be known more for his contributions that will outweigh the complaints against him as a player.

In 2010 the Chicago Blackhawks led by Jonathan Toews ended their championship drought by defeating the Philadelphia Flyers. Jonathan Toews was also awarded the Conn Smythe Trophy as the MVP of the playoffs. He was the first Blackhawk player to win the award since it was established in the playoffs. He was the second youngest player to win the Conn Smythe Award behind Patrick Roy. As well as the youngest captain to win that award also. Age is just a number. Your skills and the support surrounding you will make anything possible.

You <u>lack the time</u> that is almost everyone's excuse. *"My days are swifter than a runner; they flee away, they see no good"* (Job 9:25). If you got time to wake up and get ready for school. Or play your favorite videogame, not to mention play with your friends. You have basic Time Management skills. This is where Time Management becomes important. Time Management skills can be learned at any stage in life. It is actually an ongoing process. When you have an idea about your priorities you start making a better effort to organize the time you have to reach your goals. If you analyze the time you spend doing things you can find pockets of free time that you could use to do other things in your life. And you can find better ways to get what you need done if you focus your efforts a certain way. Then you can plan how to set time tables to get a number of things accomplished. The balancing act becomes easier when you really master managing time. Some tasks can be accomplished in a short period of time while others will take awhile. If it's really important you will find a way to deal with that situation.

My protégé was trying to figure out how to balance responsibilities in school to meet deadlines for assignments and applications. I told him he had the basics of time management already as an Acolyte. At the beginning of service we are in the church taking care of preparations depending on the type of service it is. So he already had his time budgeted to get things done. He knew how long it took to get ready to come to church in the morning. He knew how long it took to get vested. How long it took to set the readings and light the candles. As well as when there is incense used how long it took to light the coals prior to use.

After going over that it became easier to explain how to balance the time to get things done for school. Knowing his own habits he can figure out how much time to devote to other activities. Some activities will take little effort. And some will take more work. When he figured out where everything fit the rest will fall into place as needed. Time Management skills are based on your priorities. The better you balance your priorities the better your skills will become.

You might come from <u>questionable circumstances</u>. You may be in a situation that may lead to questions as to whether or not you are up to the task at hand. *Gideon answered him, "But sir, if the LORD is with us, why then has all this happened to us"* (Judg. 6:13). And conditions surrounding you may not be the most ideal. Regardless of the circumstances or obstacles that are in your path, you can still fulfill a purpose in life for the better. Not everyone is a saint. And not everyone comes from the most ideal backgrounds in life. Whatever has happened so be it. Everything that happens in your life good or bad plays a factor in your life. Treat all situations that you encounter as a learning experience and not a crutch. Learn as much as you can to help shape a better future for yourself.

The Israelites were being oppressed by the Midianites and the Amalekites (Judg. 6-8). An angel of the LORD appeared to Gideon and said that the LORD was with him. Gideon's response was the above quote stating if it's true why are they in this mess? Gideon had not only doubts that God was with him; he also doubted his own ability to achieve success. As his story unfolds Gideon was gradually empowered by God to successfully lead his people out of the strife they were under. Gideon needed proof and reproofing that assured him God was with him. And afterwards he was successful.

Another example is Jephthah. He was initially rejected because of his background. But then he was called to aid his people to aid in battling the Ammonites. *"...Are you not the very ones who rejected me and drove me out of my father's house? So why do you come to me now when you are in trouble"* (Judg. 11:7). Being initially rejected by a group of people can lead to some issues that make relationships rough. However keep your ego in check as much as possible and avoid carrying a grudge into a situation. Whatever power and authority you are given handle it with care. Make clear and sound judgments that resolve situations instead of creating more problems. Again it is not how you start it is how you finish. Your origins may not be ideal for what people want. However don't let that stop you from doing what you need to do.

I grew up in a housing project in the 1980's during the height of the Crack era. It was a scary and most often a violent period. Thankfully that wasn't the only constant in my life. Good role models surrounding me either in school or church helped with providing a better influence. There was with all relationships rough patches and differences in opinions. But in the end it was easy to avoid some of the negative trappings because of my involvement in positive things.

You might believe you have <u>poor communication skills</u>. During his calling Moses would say to God he isn't a good speaker. *"O my Lord, I have never been eloquent, neither in the past nor even now that you have spoken to your servant; but I am slow of speech and slow of tongue"* (Ex. 4:10). Leaders must be able to communicate well to those following them. In this case God responded by telling Moses to tell his brother Aaron what to say and that Aaron will speak to the people on his behalf. For the duration of the journey Aaron would address the Israelites on behalf of Moses. God would speak to Moses. And then Moses would pass on the word for Aaron to address the people.

You don't have to be an eloquent speaker to be effective in a group. You sometimes don't have to be a good speaker. Instead of thinking of something spectacular to say just keep it simple and make it plain. People will get it. And if not try and do a better job in explaining it so it becomes clearer next time. If you lack the ability to speak well take the time to know your group and find out the best way to talk to them. Some need detailed info and some don't. So take the time to find out what people really want from you and go from there. Then work to adopt a speaking style that will work for everyone.

You might feel <u>unfit</u> to handle the job. During the call of Moses he felt unfit to handle the task set before him. *"O my Lord, please send someone else"* (Ex. 4:13). It is natural if you don't feel up to the task at hand so you wish someone else had been called. It probably is true that there is someone better than you. But you are in the position for a reason. So do what you can with what you have and try to work well with others. You may not know where you fit right away in a situation. Give it time you will find your bearings and it probably will turn out you did have what it took to handle the task given to you and are where you need to be. Keep at whatever it is you are doing and endure to the end.

You may feel a level of <u>unbelief</u>. After God revealed his plan to Moses on how to free his people from Egyptian rule, Moses had doubts that the people would believe him. *"But supposed they do not believe me or listen to me of listen to me"* (Exodus 4:1). God would give him a way to show proof that all what happened was true. You may wonder if anyone will follow or listen to what you have to say. Leadership is not always an easy job. It is a business where you need to sell the idea you have and get people to buy into it. Some will go along with it. Others may take convincing. But in either case stay the course. Remain true to your task and the goals set for it. Perseverance is important.

You might <u>lack the experience</u>. Claiming to be inexperienced is not much of an excuse. As long as you treat your encounters as a learning experience you will gain more knowledge and understanding of a situation. *"The beginning of wisdom is this: Get wisdom. Though it cost all you have, get understanding"* (Prov. 4:7 NIV). Sometimes the wet behind the ears puppy has more going on than the old warhorse. It is real easy to be outclassed by the veteran 'been there done that' person.

They can talk all they want about what they have done in the past. And how they can handle what may come easier than you because of their "experience". Please note they are talking in past tense. The world is constantly changing. What your parents and grandparents probably dealt with around your age, may not be completely what you are dealing with. So they can advise you to some degree but there are still a number of unknown variables to consider. And you need to be able to balance past history with what may benefit the present and future. Take the advice and apply it the best way you can to a situation.

Ben Carson the famous surgeon retells a story in his book "Gifted Hands" about a trip to Australia in the 1980's that was a major help to him. Bryant Stokes kept trying to sell him on the idea of going to Australia claiming the trip will give him a wealth of experience. Bryant stated that Ben should take a position at the teaching hospital. Ben was concerned with the travel and more importantly the racial issues. Ben Carson was concerned about dealing with problems such as Apartheid and segregation in terms of "white only" places.

However he was constantly bombarded with images on TV suggesting taking a trip to Australia. He then talked it over with his wife and they did research. So his wife went to the library and checked things out. Note this is the 1980's so internet was not widely used for information as it is now, or accessible. It turned out that the race issue he was concerned with was abolished in 1968. Long story short the trip provided him with a wealth of knowledge and improved his reputation as surgeon making him the man to see. His skills became well known due to the work he performed during that trip. *"Buy truth, and do not sell it; buy wisdom, instruction, and understanding"* (Prov. 23:23).

Those were a handful of areas of inadequacy you may feel when approached to do something. It is ok to feel you are not up to the task. Before you throw your hands up and quit take a moment. Seek advice whenever possible. And above all as believers in God take your concerns to him and he will help you. Honestly evaluate your situation and pray on it. God will supply you with the help you need to handle the task.

"Do not worry about anything, but in everything by prayer and supplication with thanksgiving let your requests be made known to God" (Phil. 4:6).

According to the dictionary the basic definition of a leader is: One who leads or conducts; a guide; commander. A little further the definition of lead is: to go ahead of so as to show the way. So essentially it is someone who is at the forefront of something. In the end the conclusion is someone who is guiding others on their way. Let us take it a step further and use a biblical example. Here is a good biblical description for a leader. *"For a bishop, as God's steward, must be blameless; he must not be arrogant or quick-tempered or addicted to wine or violent or greedy for gain; but he must be hospitable, a lover of goodness, prudent, upright, devout, and self-controlled"* (Titus 1:7, 8).

Obviously not everyone is going to become a church leader let alone a bishop. However this is about individual growth and leadership building. You can take the qualities of leadership positions and add that to your personality. In this way you avoid more scrutiny because you are living a better lifestyle. The focus becomes less on your personal life and more on what you do as a person.

In this scripture there are both positive and negative traits we can examine. From that we can begin to find ways to be presentable as a leader that hopefully will live a decent life without possible scandal. There are eleven examples listed in this biblical text aside from blameless. There are seven positive rules of conduct. And five negative rules to avoid. As the saying goes "accentuate the positives, eliminate the negatives." Careful examination of the rules you may note that focusing on the positive rules counters the negative ones. The positive rules are: blameless, hospitable, lover of goodness, prudent, upright, devout, and self-controlled. The negative rules are: arrogant, quick-tempered, addicted to wine, violent, and greedy for gain. Let's examine the terms from the text.

Being <u>blameless</u> can also mean you are accountable for your own actions. *"The righteousness of the blameless keeps their ways straight, but the wicked fall by their own wickedness"* (Prov. 11:5). If you plan to live a responsible life then you will check behavior that will likely get you in trouble at the door. And in this way you build a positive reputation and people are likely to believe your story when you start discussing what you are about. A major part of growth as an individual is taking responsibility for your actions whether good or bad. Perception is reality to some. So the reputation and image you project will reflect you more than whatever you say about yourself.

Being confident and having a high opinion is not a problem. But not keeping your ego in check is what begins to describe being <u>arrogant</u>. *"As it is, you boast in your arrogance, all such boasting is evil"* (Jam. 4:16). When you start thinking too highly of yourself and your abilities that is a problem. Avoid being too loud about what it is you do. No one likes a person with a swell head. Keep in mind people don't like people with huge egos let alone people who talk down to them. When people think they are being talked down to it feels like their intelligence was insulted. Once insulted no one will listen or care to know what you are about. And no one likes someone who brags about everything and talks about themselves like they are God's gift to the world. This can be overcome thankfully. When you make an effort to check your ego at the door to work with others, opportunities will open for you.

A person with a short fuse and is <u>quick-tempered</u> is not healthy to be around. *"Whoever is slow to anger has great understanding, but one who has a hasty temper exalts folly"* (Prov. 14:29). They are a ticking time bomb waiting to go off at a moment's notice. And that is never a good thing. People who know someone who have a short temper will likely know how to push those buttons to make them look bad. And the person who has a short fuse will fall into many traps that will make things worse. This will lead to a bad reputation and make it harder to attract people to work with you. Hot heads get burned quicker in a situation. This can be overcome with exercising calmness in a situation. You may not always have a calm mind and a clear head. But if you take a moment to examine a situation from a variety of angles, you may find a solution that will not result in hair pulling.

Drinking a lot of alcohol is not a good habit to have. Consuming alcohol impairs judgment. So becoming <u>addicted to wine</u> is not a good thing. *"Wine is a mocker, strong drink a brawler, and whoever is led astray by it is not wise"* (Prov. 20:1). And it amplifies certain behaviors. Drinking leads to a decrease in solid decision making skills. Depending on how much you drink you will gradually become irrational for a time until the alcohol wears off. It can also lead to violent and lewd behavior. You don't want to be involved with behavior that will get you into trouble. And heavy drinking of alcohol will likely lead to trouble you may not care to be involved with. If you wish to exercise good judgment skills and decent decision making ability that means avoiding the bottle. Drinking is only good for a distraction and it keeps you from dealing with whatever situation that needs your attention. Drinking does not solve problems it masks them. To truly deal with a situation means actually facing it and coming to terms with it. On a side note while discussing this part of the verse during Acolyte Practice concerns about drug use came up in the group discussion. The kids talked about worries and dangers of drug use.

You probably heard the saying "violence leads to more violence". With that said avoid being <u>violent</u> as much as possible. *"The violent entice their neighbors, and lead them in a way that is not good"* (Prov. 16:29). As a kid I remember hearing a parent say to their child 'if someone hits you hit them back'. On the one hand the parent was likely saying for their child to defend themselves and fight back. However, fighting can escalate to something worse if not careful. While studying Martial Arts, the rule is self defense. And the use of violence is as a last resort. And please note attacking someone might lead to more attacks on you. What started out as a simple dispute between two people can escalate into a huge brawl with a group of people. That's how wars get started sometimes. So be careful of how you handle beefs and disputes with one another. Some disputes may end up leading to a fight. However do what you can to resolve a beef before it escalates to people walking about with an all consuming hate for each other.

It is ok to be ambitious. It is ok to want things. But do not let it exceed your grasp because being greedy for gain is not a good thing. Reaching for a goal is one thing. But trying to grasp for more than your fair share is wrong. *"Those who are greedy for unjust gain make trouble for their households, but those who hate bribes will live"* (Prov. 15:27). Lack of direction and decision making will lead to you mishandling things and likely lose control of what's going on. *"Do not wear yourself out to get rich; be wise enough to desist"* (Prov. 23:4). You may win big in the short term but will likely lose out in the long run. Success will come to you. But you need to exercise patience and focus the right way on your goals.

Being welcoming to people is important. Practice being a hospitable person and inviting to people but do it in a careful manner. *"Be hospitable to one another without complaining"* (1 Pet. 4:9). You never know what you have surrounding you until you take the moment to find out. The solution to the situation may be staring you in the face but you did not take the moment to find out. So be welcoming to one another and whatever you are struggling with may be resolved because of the people you encountered recently. When you think you lack the resources for a situation. You might find a hidden gem that is the answer for you.

You aspire for excellence so being a lover of goodness is a positive. If you are focusing on honor and great quality, you must love what is good. *"You are good and do good; teach me your statutes"* (Ps. 119:68). With that said you will constantly look to do what is right and just so people will view you in a positive image. This means shedding any baggage that may hold you back so you can truly do well for others.

A sharp mind is always important so feel encouraged being a prudent person. *"The clever do all things intelligently, but the fool displays folly"* (Prov. 13:16). A person who takes a moment to think things through will likely have a better idea of what is going on and how to handle things. It does not have to be a long contemplative act. However a smart person will likely think before they leap so they make a better choice in planning their next move. A smart person will have a decent, calculated way of approaching a situation. And the approach will likely keep others from getting into trouble because the individual will come off as sounding like a rational person who is trustworthy. And you want people to trust and buy into whatever you are saying.

Someone who is <u>upright</u> is usually honest and just. *"The righteousness of the upright saves them, but the treacherous are taken captive by their schemes"* (Prov. 11:6). Being upright is similar to being blameless. Because someone who believes in being honest and just are likely to do what is right for themselves and others will find ways to avoid trouble. When you focus on doing what is right you live without regrets. *"The highway of the upright avoids evil; those who guard their way preserve their lives"* (Prov. 16:17). When you scheme to do wrong that is when the trouble starts. When you do wrong you have to now keep your lies consistent. When you do right by others and yourself things are less complicated.

There is calmness to a person that is <u>devout</u>. *"He was a devout man who feared God with all his household; he gave alms generously to the people and prayed constantly to God"* (Acts 10:2). They tend to have a quiet focused nature about themselves. In addition to that they are also serious about how they approach things in life. There tends to be a built in trust with someone of that nature. Becoming devout is an ongoing process. And like all honest living it is a constant practice. When you make an effort to commit to that lifestyle there will be challenges but you will have a path that will keep you honest and people will consistently have trust in you.

Lack of any control is never a good thing. You will need to be <u>self-controlled</u> as much as possible. *"Like a city breached, without walls, is one who lacks self-control"* (Prov. 25:28). A rational person has not only control of their ego. They also know how to control their temper as well. There will be times where things will test your patience. However that is not the time to lose control. As stated before a rational person exhibits a level of control. So in whatever is going on do what you can to remain calm. Perseverance is crucial. *"Whoever is slow to anger has great understanding, but one who has a hasty temper exalts folly"* (Prov. 14:29).

In examining calling it is easy to feel inadequate for the job. The goal of this chapter is to face whatever reasons you feel make you unfit for the job. Once you identify why you may feel that way. The next step is to find ways to overcome that. Life at times will throw you some challenges. After you find reasons as to where you are lacking the next step is to find solutions to help you achieve your goals. That is where team building comes into play. This however will not be discussed here. That will be discussed in the third chapter "Play to your Strengths".

After discussing inadequacies in this chapter we went on to describe leadership both from the dictionary and the bible while using the verse from Titus. There are seven positive rules and five negative ones. Being self-controlled, a lover of goodness, and blameless will generally be constant in life. At times you will need on varying degrees to be prudent, upright, devout, as well as hospitable. The situations in life vary how these commands if studied and practiced will help you get through many of the challenges you will face. And focusing on the positives will help you avoid the troubles that come from the negative commands. Self control when practiced will keep you out of trouble. And a sound mind that is upright and prudent will help you balance the situation to allow yourself to stay out of trouble as well. The other positive commands are a bonus.

We are all flawed in some ways so you can never truly eliminate the negatives. They will always be around in some form or another. But we can focus on the positive qualities. Recognize and work towards them. All the while recognizing the negatives and finding ways to avoid them. As long as you treat life constantly as a learning experience you should have little problem being able to find ways to apply these rules to daily activities.

I am naturally a church going person and a sports fan. In sports when it comes to team leaders outside of management and coaching staff, you have the Team Captain. The Team Captain is usually the most identifiable member of the team. The person is either the lead scorer or the person that is to a degree a leader in the locker room. I prefer the latter. When a team is struggling that tests the skills of the leader. The person will now have to try and motivate their team to victory not only by words but by actions as well. And win or lose the team leader has to set an example.

In a church setting leadership takes on many dimensions. It is not just about how you speak. It is also about how you carry yourself and how you treat others. Sometimes a church setting can be very hostile as if it is a privileged social club. That becomes a turn off for many visitors. The structure top to bottom has to be inviting to people. The established leaders need to set the tone. And the support base needs to follow suit. With decent communication this can be done. However keep in mind the people surrounding you. Some are paid employees, while others are part time volunteers with obligations outside the church setting. Balancing duties within the church and taking care of personal matters need to be a priority.

Allow me to introduce myself. Members of my church know me as a longtime Acolyte that became their first ever Verger. However I started out originally in the Boy Scouts. As a kid I used to watch the commercials on television about them. I joined as a Cub Scout. A group was started at the Community Center that didn't go anywhere. Someone later on told my parents about Cub Scouts in a nearby church.

Roughly two years later I kept noticing the Acolytes at the church setting up things before service. One thing led to another and I joined the Acolytes. Two years after joining the Acolytes I left the Boy Scouts. I had issues with certain people so after leaving decided not to join another Scout troop. However despite not being involved in the scouts I actually became more of a Scout from what I was doing in the Acolytes. At that time I was a Webelos Scout in the Cub Scouts when I joined the Acolytes. Upon joining the group I was introduced to the leader of the group the late Mr. Webster B. Tapper. He would die five years after I joined. But the lessons learned from him I still use today.

The group leader took me under his wing. Gradually progressing through the ranks within the ministry of the Acolyte program from

Acolyte to Altar Server and finally Senior Acolyte it was preparation for becoming to a degree a leader. Originally when the Acolyte Ministry was established it was preparation for becoming a Priest. But over time things changed and the reasons for things being done got adjusted. Just think the Levites during the Exodus had a specific role (Num. 1:48-54). Then the Levites were reassigned by King David later on (1 Chr. 23:28-32). As an Acolyte you learn areas of the church, and about the items used during service. As an Altar Server you work closely with the clergy during services. And you learn better the mechanics of the worship service which indirectly teaches you Time Management skills. A Senior Acolyte is someone who is well rounded and can easily handle duties of both Acolyte and Altar Server.

During my college days I was involved in the local Chapter of the National Society of Black Engineers. First I was appointed as the Ujima committee chair, within the chapter, which was liaison to the local Alumni Chapter. Then I was elected as Chapter President the following year. Actually I was elected as a Vice President but ended up taking over after the President elect was a no show. During that time I learned how to delegate responsibility as well as deal with deadlines and paperwork. While President my role was to plan events, activities, trips to conferences as well as appointed committee chairs.

After that period I was back at church. Around that time I experienced personal tragedies. Following that and coming to terms with them, my predecessor Cecil who ran the Acolytes picked me to speak in church on Youth Sunday in October 2000. It was a tall order mainly because it ended up being two weeks after the weeklong Festival for our church. My Rector led the services that week preaching for the majority of them. Cecil preached at Youth Night. It was a good thing I went to it. That month I was drawing a blank on what to do. Following his sermon the idea came to me. The sermon that night was discussing people who fell away. My situation echoed that easily. So that became the topic.

After delivering my sermon Cecil announced he was leaving the group and handing everything to me. I went home and with a doomed look on my face told my mother that my mentor was leaving the Acolytes and handing over leadership to me. Unfortunately due to my situation at work I was unable to follow through with running the group for roughly two years. So it was left to others until I got back. Upon returning I assumed the responsibilities as requested of me. I came back in 2004. There was an uphill battle because when I got back the person I left in charge was not there and others who had nothing to do with the group tried to take over. Ironically they called Cecil for help and he said it was in my hands. After about a year of struggle people finally left it in my hands and I began restoring the group to where it should be.

In 2005 a Verger from a local church (St. Andrew's) came to my church to recruit someone to be Verger here. He was recently installed at his church. He had a talk with the President of the Guild and complained about how he was the only established Verger in the Bronx. The President suggested to the person that he do something about it. That is when my Rector (Head Priest at the church) was contacted for permission to come to our church on a recruitment mission. Canon Reid our then Rector was open to the situation. That morning one of the Chalice Bearers (in recent years Chalice Bearers were changed to be Eucharistic Ministers) asked me what I knew about Vergers. I said not much, and he went on to tell me about speaking to his wife that I would make a good one. Shortly after that conversation that Verger walked in and headed to where my priest was standing.

During the course of the service the Verger was constantly focused on me trying to ask questions. My focus was on the service and taking care of things. It was not until announcements that he made it clear that he was there to recruit someone to be a Verger at the church. At the end of service while I was talking to the acolytes he chased me down and started asking questions. First question was how long I have been an acolyte with my Rector. I said 16 years with the Rector and 18 years overall at the church. Despite my lack of interest in the ministry he kept suggesting I was a good fit for it. It was a hard sell for me especially since the person recruiting me looked old enough to be my father.

No one has ever held that title at my church so there was no one to give me advice about it. The basic knowledge I had about Vergers was people dressed up like college professors on Graduation Day carrying staffs. Again with a doomed look on my face told my mother I was recruited to be the first ever Verger at my church. Given my reluctance to embrace the calling to the Ministry of Vergers, Cecil came up with a suggestion. He said if I feel it will hinder my ability to run the Acolytes then it is best to avoid becoming a Verger.

Interestingly that month the Vergers Guild was having a conference. And it fell on the week I was on vacation. My mindset was still 'no' even while flying out to the event. My first Verger conference was in Tennessee and it was an awkward experience. Not to mention I went there sick after being caught in a rain storm a few days earlier. In addition we were in the mountains. So I'm sick and in a cold mountain region for a conference. Not fun.

But over time it proved to be a rewarding experience, despite whatever reservations on my part for going initially. When interacting with others who were at the conference. It turns out I really did have the tools needed to follow through with what was needed of me. My wilderness journey proved fruitful and gave me clarity and focus.

There was naturally a fair amount of ignorance about the situation in the beginning. And really didn't feel I was up to dealing with that. Given the considerable age gap there was a strong feeling of being too young. And at the Verger conferences my 'peers' were more mature looking than me which at times was intimidating. But that was just on the surface. The conferences I attended for the most part were like a family gathering. One of my favorite comments from a visiting priest in my early days as Verger was when he said "You can't be a Verger you don't have any grey or white hair." He said that jokingly though.

I may not be as mature looking as my peers however age is just a number. When it appeared that there was a possible lack of experience.

It turns out that the structure setup to train Acolytes at my church was preparation for leadership positions within the church. And provided the foundation needed to perform many of the duties of a Verger.

Once it became clear that the Ministry of Vergers was a progression of the Acolytes Ministry, the mindset became finding ways to incorporate the ministry into what was already being done at church. Unless people have been to the cathedral they probably have no idea what a Verger is. The ministry itself is probably exclusive to the Episcopal Church. And to the parents of Acolytes at the church it was important to explain quickly that I was not going anywhere. The main thought for some was that it meant being at the cathedral so assuring people that wasn't the case had to be explained.

When it comes to being a Verger you tend to be a combination of all the lay ministries within the church. This ministry is a combination of: Lay Reader, Usher, Sexton, Altar Guild, among other groups. The Acolyte program at my church is blended with Altar Guild duties. Because of the length of time I spent within the Acolytes there was gradually a built in understanding of worship services. Along with a working knowledge of how things worked and an attitude of treating everything as a learning process, moving forward was easy. However knowledge and experience means nothing if there is a lack of a working relationship with the priest. And more than ever when a priest visits the church they immediately direct all questions and concerns to me.

The Ministry of Vergers is an appointed position within the church. The origins of this ministry trace back to Medieval England. A Verger is dubbed 'Protector of the Procession'. When looking up Verger in the dictionary you find two possible definitions. One is church official who handles the interior of the church. The other is that of mace bearer. At a conference when we gather for the group photo there is usually a difference in the style of robes worn there.

Some Vergers wear a modified academic gown which has lappets hanging from the shoulder area. While others wear a sleeveless gown called the chimere (pronounced sha-mir). This gown does not have lappets hanging from it. The lappets hanging from the gown are either plain or have the same colored trim as the gown. For example green trim on the gown will have green trim on the lappets. The lappets on the gown serves as a reminder of the fact that Vergers moved about an area with books and other paraphernalia tied to them. The color of the trim on the individual's gown represents the church they serve. Think Captain America, his costume is the colors of the American flag. The gown also protected the wearer from cold weather. I always tell people my gown is like a trench coat.

The gown I wear is a chimere gown. It is a gown that is worn over a cassock. In my case it is a black cassock. My church colors according to the Rector were red and blue. The original idea was that the trim on my gown would be red. This was so that if the acolytes wore red cassocks we would match and if they wore black we would still match. When the date of my Installation Service was set it was shortly after my birthday. So upon seeing my gown prior to the service I was surprised to see green trim. Then again my birthday is St. Patrick's Day. Maybe it is a hidden birthday reference.

A verger is not limited to wearing a gown with just a specific trim color. They can add patches of the Guild they are affiliated with and the diocese they are from among other church related patches. A collar can be worn as well. There are also hats that can be worn too which is optional.

For hats there is the Oxford Bonnet and Canterbury Cap. The main reason I got a bonnet was to cover my head when it is cold outside. There were a number of funerals one year during the winter time. My body would be fairly warm due to the gown but my head would be cold while leading the body outside the church. Given that my role in the church is as a part time volunteer, this meant still having to report to my regular job for a paycheck. The last thing I want to say to my boss is that I got sick doing extracurricular activities.

Like a Bishop, the Verger also carries a staff of office. The staff carried by a Verger is called a virge with longer variations being called a beadle pole. Originally the staff we used was a weapon to protect participants of the service. Again one of the dictionary definitions is mace bearer. The picture displayed is of me after the March of Witness on Palm Sunday.

Like the angel that God appoints to protect the Israelites during the Exodus, the Verger led the way for everyone. *"I am going to send an angel in front of you, to guard you on the way and to bring you to the place that I have prepared"* (Ex. 23:20). The staff was used to clear the way of anyone or animals that would disrupt the procession. The staff is now used more as a symbolic reminder of the past and is made for less combative means.

These days the Verger assists the Clergy in planning services and helps deal with preparations for the service at church. There is the belief that Vergers tell the Clergy what to do. But that is misleading. The Verger follows the order of worship services as dictated by the Clergy. So in the end it is the Clergy that empowers the Verger in their duties. As stated before the ministry of Verger is an appointed position so a person serves in that capacity with the approval of the Clergy. In the same way that Jesus says his authority comes from the Father (Jn. 5:19-24), it is the same for Vergers. The Vergers are commissioned by the Clergy to serve in the Parishes and Cathedrals.

The focus of this chapter was to show examples of overcoming whatever inadequacies you may feel is holding you back. Whatever doubts and fears you have pray on it. Turn your weakness into strength. *"My grace is sufficient for you, for power is made perfect in weakness"* (2 Cor. 12:9).

Also when you take an honest examination of yourself you may find that the tools needed for the job was already there for use. The skills may not be obvious at the start but over time it may become present. As stated before make sure whatever calling you receive is an honest one. There are people who see potential in what you can do. And there are others that will exploit you for whatever means suit them. Even if people use you for the wrong means it can still be used to your advantage. As long as you know the difference between right and wrong you will be able to find a way through a situation. *"I hereby command you: Be strong and courageous; do not be frightened or dismayed, for the LORD your God is with you wherever you go"* (Josh. 1:9).

CHAPTER TWO

Words have Power

Elihu son of Barachel the Buzite answered: "I am young in years, and you are aged; therefore I was timid and afraid to declare my opinion to you. I said, 'Let days speak, and many years teach wisdom' (Job 32:6, 7).

This passage is taken from the book of Job. For a time during the course of that book the conversation involved Job and his friends. After a lot of back and forth Job gives what is pretty much his closing argument declaring he is not guilty of any wrong doing that resulted in his suffering. Once things got silent and there was no response Elihu begins speaking.

Elihu for awhile was listening and at first not sure what to say given he was clearly younger than the group speaking. He later finds his voice and begins addressing the group voicing his opinions. It is open to debate whether or not he really added to the conversation. But he did provide input.

It is not easy speaking to a group of people. As a kid, youth, young adult, or even young at heart it will always be a challenge. It can also be intimidating when dealing with a group that is more mature than you. However it can be overcome. First off do not panic. Second take a moment and feel out the crowd. The more you know your audience the easier it will be for you. The rest will come to you in time just keep at it. You will find your voice. Moses (Ex. 4:10-15) and Jeremiah (Jer. 1:6, 7) didn't know how to speak either. And yet they found their voice.

In Jeremiah, God calls him to speak to the people. Jeremiah clearly states that he is a boy. But God states that despite Jeremiah being a boy. Jeremiah was still up for the task regardless of the lack of experience. God was going to supply Jeremiah with all he needed to do the job at hand.

In the first chapter of this book when discussing calling, Moses was brought up. The focus of that section of the chapter was overcoming inadequacies. When God called Moses to lead his people Moses points out he is a terrible speaker (Ex. 4:10). God points out that he gives speech to people and will teach Moses how to speak. Moses still doubts he is up to it and God suggests letting Aaron speak for him. God will speak to Moses and then Moses will tell Aaron what needs to be said.

In the Gospel of Luke, Jesus is discussing how to react to future persecutions. Jesus gives these words: *"For I will give you words and wisdom that none of your adversaries will be able to resist or contradict"* (Lk. 21:15 NIV). Just as God was assuring Moses and Jeremiah that all the tools they needed to address the crowds would be provided for them. Jesus also assures his disciples that when the time comes whatever they need will be supplied to them.

This chapter is about learning the right way to use words. And also how to speak in public whether it is in conversation or towards crowds. Learning how to speak to crowds may be intimidating at first. But there are ways to overcome situations like this that may at first seem challenging. First off remember that we are all human with the same if not similar abilities. We bleed the same blood and put on clothes the same way. Our concerns and fears are at times similar as well. In breaking the ice take a moment to know the material you are trying to present. And then learn a bit about your audience for starters.

When you are around friends how is the conversation like? When interacting with other groups of people what is your approach? While in college I attended a class called "Public Speaking", the professor stated that one of the biggest fears of people is public speaking. The professor was a Drama teacher so he had acted out how to speak sometimes in class. And he came off natural like he was holding a one sided conversation with you. The lessons he taught us didn't sink in right away with me. However the fundamentals he tried to teach came to the surface when I was learning how to speak publicly.

One of the first things I remembered was he made a comment people fear speaking more than death. There are a number of reasons to fear speaking in public. A lesson he taught was on display when I watched Myrlie Evers-Williams former President of the NAACP speaking at the National Society of Black Engineers convention in Kansas City, Missouri (1999). It was Opening Session. And just as she was coming to speak the person introducing her requested that the lights be turned on so she could see us.

It is probably a scary notion to look into the crowd while you speak. But the basic rule when talking to someone is to look at them. So looking into a crowd is not a bad thing. When you talk make sure you know the topic you are talking about. And have an idea what type of audience you have. True story Mrs. Williams forgot her speech on the way to the event. This meant creating on the spot another speech. Given she was the Keynote Speaker, she was the main event. With that said she took in what was going on around her.

She incorporated the events of the Opening Session, the name of the organization, and her own personal background into a solid speech. She was invited by the National Society of Black Engineers to speak. The National Society of Black Engineers is a professional society. She clearly is not in the engineering field. Despite that it is likely before agreeing to speak at an event hosted by a group she looked up background info on them so that she matched their goals. And there is usually a theme that goes with the convention. The more of an idea you have of the people surrounding you the better you will likely communicate with them. In the end it was a memorable speech she did.

My protégé who I trained in the Acolytes takes after me a lot. During Youth Sunday he is usually asked to speak in church. And as usual he borrows from our conversations or heavily quotes me in his sermons. Well he was tapped to speak one Sunday. So he was stuck because he was preoccupied with other things at school. After service we looked at the readings for next week for ideas.

We looked at the Gospel reading first. The reading was Matthew 6:25-34. We read the text. After reading I stayed quiet and waited for his reaction. When he clearly was not sure what to do, I gave him a suggestion. The text discussed not worrying. However I put another spin on that topic. The idea was to not focus on the text itself, but to discuss not worrying. For example take the challenges he faced and how he dealt with them. He came up with three real life stories. The sermon was a success.

And it led to a number of testimonials that morning. The Interim Priest (we were in between priests because the previous Rector had left) mentioned an issue they were dealing with. And a couple got up and discussed long standing financial problems that ultimately got resolved. Also the friend he mentions in one of his stories appeared in church that morning as well. So it ended up being an interesting day. At the end of one of the stories he points out that I taught him something. He got that out the first time. But the second time around in the following service he really got into it so he didn't say my name during the second time. He was mad about it. But I told him it did not matter. If people could not tell he got it from me that was their problem.

The two stories shared about Public Speaking had a purpose. As stated with Myrlie Evers-Williams she forgot her prepared speech and had to make one up when she got there. Naturally given her experience it was not a stretch to come up with something on the way to speaking. I do not know how much time prior to the convention she had in preparing a speech after being invited. However as stated before it is likely that she would have taken the time to find out about a group so the speech would match what the goals and aims of the group is. With an understanding of the group it is easier to guess how to better connect with the audience afterwards.

In the case of my protégé he has been speaking for awhile. At that point in time he was dry in terms of ideas. So after reading the lessons for that day it was easier to figure out what to do next. He has been speaking to the same crowd for awhile so there was an automatic familiarity with each other. With that said he just had to be comfortable with what he was talking about. Because the conversation about the verses sparked an idea to tell stories, he fell into a comfort level where the sermon was based on something he knew he could discuss. Find an area you are comfortable talking about in a subject and things will work out.

That is fine in cases with people with experience speaking. But that does not help someone who has never spoken to a crowd or is uneasy about speaking. Here are some basics that I learned that could help you deal with speaking to crowds. Given what I discussed about Myrlie Evers-Williams and my protégé some of the items will seem like review.

Basic advice anyone will give you is be yourself. If you are comfortable with what you are doing it will not look good while doing it. In being yourself be original. You do not have to act like anyone else. Look at people when you are talking to them. When you do that it is easier to read if they are following what you are saying by the way they are reacting. If they look unclear about what you said that should lead you to go into better detail. That is just starters for how to carry yourself when you speak.

When it comes to speaking make sure you have an understanding of the material you are discussing. Being in a situation where you don't know what you are talking about is anything but pleasant. Take a moment and understand who you are talking to. Age is not always a factor when talking about certain issues. And if you are carrying yourself a certain way, being in a situation where you address a younger or older crowd should not be a problem. Attitude will carry you through.

There is nothing wrong with being humorous while speaking. There are some people who add humor to either break the ice in talking. Or just on occasion to lighten the mood while speaking. That is a double edged sword. Depending on the subject a joke can either help or hurt a situation. And a joke could overwhelm the subject where people might remember the joke better than the topic you presented. Reactions to jokes are unpredictable so be aware of that and balance the topic to allow moments of humor. If you are too serious in the beginning a joke will catch others off guard.

My former Rector shared a situation where on Good Friday they had guest preachers. One preacher gave a good sermon. Another preacher came up and had the crowd going and reacting to what he said. This made the previous preacher feel like he did a bad job. However in looking back the previous preacher had more substance in his speech compared to the other. Worry more about the getting your point across as opposed to crowd reactions. Interesting enough posts I make on social media sites don't get major reactions in terms of 'likes'. But a number of people have walked up to me later on saying they appreciate what I do and to keep at it. In other words do not concern yourself with popularity. Just concern yourself with making sure the work you did is satisfying to you. The rest will take care of itself.

You do not have to be over the top when you are speaking. Keep it simple. When I am in a situation at church having to read lessons in place of someone who is missing, the approach is very basic. After announcing what is being read that is followed by a pause. That gets me mentally ready to read. After glancing at what is being read, that is followed by pacing with pausing at commas and stopping at periods and semicolons. People come up and say they are blown away by how I read. And it was a simple approach. Play it safe and make it plain. Everything else will work itself out.

When addressing crowds. As stated before looking at people helps out things. The fear will always be there to an extent when speaking to people. However they are flesh and blood just like you. Speaking like many things is an individual experience. Finding a comfortable way to deal with crowds is up to you. Once you are able to deal with that obstacle the rest will fall into place.

My first couple of times speaking to a group was a daunting task. Given my quiet nature trying to talk to groups of people let alone crowds was a challenge at first. My former mentor helped me put together my first sermon. I understood better from him the concept of cut and paste even though at the time we were cutting actual sheets and rearranging them for my sermon. The first time out he had me first talk to a small group before getting in front the crowd. Honestly I had no idea of what I was doing at the time. However that situation helped me better organize what to do. And it helped me understand how to approach speaking in public the next time around.

As stated earlier watching Myrlie Evers-Williams speak reminded me of the "Public Speaking" class I took. Some of the lessons learned were discussed just now. Once you have a comfort level with the material you are discussing. The next step is to understand the group you are talking to. Find out what their interests are. Match the material you are talking about with what they may be interested in.

Depending on their age and viewpoints make sure you say things that will not insult their intelligence. You can indirectly offend someone. And it is not a matter of using racial slurs or calling them names. Your tone while speaking can offend someone. You can also talk about the material in a way that can rub someone the wrong way. One time in class a student gave a great presentation. But at times the way certain parts were presented it felt like your intelligence was insulted. Once someone is offended they might tune you out. So be careful with how you speak and carry yourself. Again know your audience.

The better you know your audience the better you can communicate with them. When I was developing my skills speaking in public my cues came from what Mrs. Williams and my professor did. It took awhile to develop a decent speaking style. When my predecessor was running the Acolytes he left me in charge of the group for a time before he stepped down years later. So prior to graduating from High School there was some practice in public speaking. Then after going to college and becoming Chapter President of the National Society of Black Engineers I had to learn how to conduct meetings. My speaking skills were fine tuned at this point.

Because the previous Presidents gave out Agenda sheets to know what the meetings were about I followed that pattern. But when it came to making speeches it was clear my skills at speech writing were not good. My lack of patience would not let me write a decent speech. However borrowing from the Public Speaking class I wrote outlines for the speeches. I may be bad at speech writing but am good at organizing my thoughts. The outlines kept me going in a specific direction so I reached the end the right way. Also because I am not spending time reading words it makes things easier to connecting with people while talking.

Making eye contact is important in communication. When you hold a conversation with anyone a good habit to have is looking at someone while talking to them. When the audience feels like you are engaging them they become more attentive. Some evangelists walk around the place while talking. And as they move about they are connecting more to the audience. The audience may not be listening to the message but they feel more involved in what is going on. Even if you do not move around while talking, simple things like eye contact with people go a long way. And don't be afraid to trip up on words at times. The only mistakes people notice are the ones you make obvious. So play off mistakes like that was supposed to happen and move on.

In speaking to anyone know the right way to speak to them. There is a right way and a wrong way to speak to people. Here are examples of the right and wrong way to speak to someone. *"A soft answer turns away wrath, but a harsh word stirs up anger"* (Prov. 15:1). In the book of Judges you have two similar situations involving the Judge and the men of Ephraim. The Judges were Gideon and Jephthah. One situation ended without incident while the other ended badly. In the case with Gideon after defeating the Midianites he is confronted by the Ephraimites (Judg. 8:1-3) who complain about not being involved in the fighting. Gideon could have responded in the same way and just as angrily as they were towards him. But instead of doing that he offered a peaceful solution. When he resolved the dispute with a compromise cooler heads prevailed and things calmed down.

In the case of Jephthah when the Ephraimites approached him (Judg. 12:1-7) about why they were not called to fight, a civil war happened. Jephthah unlike Gideon did not find a peaceful solution to the situation. Jephthah instead of trying to find a compromise with the angry group instead reacted badly. The group upset about not being called threatened to burn Jephthah's home down (Judg. 12:1). After Jephthah went on about his efforts and success he turned it on them asking why they want to fight him. The situation escalated to a civil war where 42,000 people were killed. Ego can make you say things you probably wouldn't have said in other circumstances. Even if you make a mistake, make the effort to correct the harm you did.

Be careful what you say out loud. It can mean the difference between helping and hurting a situation. Knowing how to speak to people is not easy. Also knowing the way to speak is equally if not extra hard. It is a constant learning experience. Even when you are not meaning harm, you can say something that can be read the wrong way. Being politically correct may help avoid hurting people. But you still need to make an effort to understand whoever you are talking to in order to avoid problems.

Also when speaking it is not just about what you say it is how you say it. You should be encouraged to speak your mind and be honest. However knowing the right way to speak at a given moment takes effort. Being "politically correct" does not relieve you of the obligation to know what is or is not offensive to someone. Politically correct terms were intended to avoid problems with people. But to truly avoid problems with other races or even other cultures you need to make an effort to reach out and understand them. When that is established you will find yourself in less awkward situations thinking you did well only to find someone was put off by what you said.

We may have the right to 'Freedom of Speech' however we should be careful how we exercise that right. Whether you are speaking to a crowd of people or holding a conversation with your friends make an effort to know your audience. *"To watch over mouth and tongue is to keep out of trouble"* (Prov. 21:23).

There was a situation during Acolyte Practice where an argument happened. There was a clear misunderstanding because the person did not get the joke that the others made. The response from my predecessor to the group involved was "Are they in your calling circle?" That comment probably seems dated. Especially since it was a famous calling plan for a phone company call MCI. When he made that comment about calling circles it clearly meant did the person understand where the others were coming from. If he did the problem would not have happened. Make sure when you communicate anything to anyone that the person or people have a clue what you are talking about.

My predecessor who ran the Acolytes liked to refer to "taming of the tongue" found in James 3:1-12. In it the writer describes how potent a loose tongue can be. Having control of your mouth can avoid disaster in the future. The writer points out that we can tame wild animals but no one can tame the tongue. *"For every species of beast and bird, of reptile and sea creature, can be tamed and has been tamed by the human species, but no one can tame the tongue—a restless evil, full of deadly poison"* (Jam. 3:7, 8). Learning to control your mouth is an ongoing process. However the goal here is to help you guard what you are saying to avoid getting into trouble. In addition to that is helping find your voice if you have not done so already.

There is a moment in the gospels where Jesus is talking about traditions with Elders. The Elders were complaining about how the Disciples were eating without washing their hands. Jesus responds with discussing how it is not what goes in your mouth that makes you unclean, but what comes out their mouths that make them unclean.

Jesus says *"What goes into someone's mouth does not defile them, but what comes out of their mouth, that is what defiles them"* (Matt. 15: 11 NIV). Before explaining the parable he makes a bathroom reference saying what goes in the mouth ends in the sewer. He then goes on to say *"But what comes out of the mouth proceeds from the heart, and this is what defiles"* (Matt. 15: 18).

The book of James says a lot about the power of the tongue. If you are not careful it will get you into a lot of trouble. Combine that with what Jesus says about what comes out the mouth can make you unclean that can also mean the need to be careful what you say. Speaking is a form of communication. And at times speaking is a form of expression. With that said be careful how you express yourself. Be yourself and speak your mind. But also be considerate of others thoughts and feelings.

The better you know them, and they know where you are coming from. The easier things will be in communicating to each other. It is what is in the inside that counts. Take an honest look at what your thoughts are when you communicate. Better yet take a look at how Jesus talks to people. He talks to a group of people a certain way. There is a certain style of speaking when he is surrounded by crowds of people as opposed to when he is around friends. And he speaks a certain way when around his critics too.

Naturally this conversation would not be complete without commenting on watching your language. *"But now you must rid yourselves of all such things as these: anger, rage, malice, slander, and filthy language from your lips"* (Col. 3:8 NIV). Early on the conversation was about pointers on how to communicate with others. Understanding the right way to possibly talk to others is a must. Also take note that when you become to a degree a public figure anything you say will likely be on record. You probably will not be a celebrity. But if you are a familiar face because of what you do in church or elsewhere you are to an extent a public figure. So using foul language in public or on social media sites can possible come back to haunt you. You never know who is listening and someone might report what you said. Be aware of the people around you at all times. That way you can avoid problems in the future.

For the record you will get emotional. And that may lead to angry comments that are harmful to others. Keep in mind once you say something it is out there. So be careful what you say, and the context of what you are saying. It will mean the difference between keeping and losing friends. Words have power in numerous ways. Words can either help or hurt others. Do not take what you do lightly. *"The mind of the righteous ponders how to answer, but the mouth of the wicked pours out evil"* (Prov. 15:28).

The first half of this chapter was all about finding your voice. Finding the courage to speak in a given situation is not easy. As a young person it could be intimidating speaking to a crowd, and probably more so when the group is older than you. Give it time. You will find your voice with effort. You will not be right all the time. And you will probably find people giving you odd looks after you ask a question or make a comment. Do not be discouraged. There are times where I get odd looks when I ask questions in a group situation. But in the end it helped me know better how to help someone out because they didn't know I needed to know certain things to help them better. You never know unless you ask. And the better you know something the easier your task will become.

As stated earlier learning the right way to speak to others is an ongoing process. So make an effort to find out how to talk to people in a way that will not be a put off. And then learn how to stay within that guideline to avoid alienating a friend. Understanding where people are coming from and allowing them to get familiar with you will go a long way in developing healthy relationships in communicating thoughts and ideas. Watch the language to avoid trouble in the future.

Along with words having power in communicating with others, let us not forget about using the bible. The bible has many uses. And we need to be aware of how to use it properly. *"Indeed, the word of God is living and active, sharper than any two-edged sword, piercing until it divides soul and spirit, joints from marrow; it is able to judge the thoughts and intentions of the heart"* (Heb. 4:12).

In the movie "The Book of Eli" Gary Oldman chases Denzel Washington across a post apocalyptic world for possession of a bible. When questioned about the point of hunting down this 'book', Gary Oldman's character goes into detail about how the words of that book have power. The bible is filled with a great deal of power. The verse from Hebrews lays claim to the bible being a sharp sword. The only offensive weapon listed in the Armor of God is the word *"...and the sword of the Spirit, which is the word of God"* (Eph. 6:17). However how we use it is just as important in possessing it. The only way we can be able to harness its power is by studying the right way to use it. And while learning to use it we must be able to make it relevant for others to benefit from it in a positive way.

Take the story of Apollos for example. Apollos appears in Acts 18:24-28.

Apollos as stated in the Acts is well versed in scripture (Acts 18:24).

However despite his skill with scripture he was lacking. *"He had been instructed in the Way of the Lord; and he spoke with burning enthusiasm and taught accurately the things concerning Jesus, though he knew only the baptism of John"* (Acts 18:25). Thankfully he was given further instruction by people who knew what he was missing (Acts 18:26). Apollos is an example of being skilled in teaching scripture. But he learned how to better teach for the benefit of others. Initially we think we know what we are doing. However we can always use further study. As they say there is room for improvement.

I must confess when approached to write a book like this there was a fair amount of reluctance. Mainly because it would require that I actually read a bible in order to apply scripture to the book properly. And my story is probably like some where a bible is in the house but seldom used. I grew up in the church and with the exception of readings on Sunday mornings I never touched the bible. After Confirmation class my mother gave me a King James Version Red Letter bible. That is a bible with Jesus' words in red. Given I hardly used that bible it is probably to this day in near mint condition with maybe some dust settled on it. There was a teen bible study group in church but I stayed away from it. The main reason was since my older sister was such a big deal at the time it felt like many people at church just tolerated me because of who I was related to. When people mainly wanted to know is how someone else is doing, that makes it hard to feel like they want you around.

My High School days was a lost period in my life trying to figure who I was and where to go. While coming to terms with painful events of the past there was an encounter with a group outside my church that was into the bible. They introduced me to the New International Version of the bible. While studying with them, the bible readings reminded me of where I was before the mess and how to get back to the needed place in order to fly right. In other words they taught me what I already knew but this time it was scripture based. Just as in the account of Luke's Gospel: *"Then he opened their minds to understand the scriptures"* (Lk. 24:45). My eyes were opened to scriptures as well. After awhile we had many disagreements fundamentally so the relationship didn't last.

Upon returning to my home church I purchased a New Revised Standard Version because that is what they were using there. Understanding my ignorance of the bible it was clear not to purchase a regular text bible. A student bible was purchased so that there was some type of guide to help in following my reading and study. Not to mention there were several reading tracks to use.

Despite the advantages to helping me get into reading the bible I was hardly reading it. But when the decision was made to start writing this book it became important to develop a reading habit with the bible to help draw more material out to better develop the book. A search for certain words and topics can only do so much for this. When the Lenten season came up my usual habits during this time is not to give up anything. It's to take an honest look at who I am and where I am going. Given it is a penitent season there is reflection involved. Hopefully coming out better than how I went in and changing for the better.

I used to have a love hate relationship with the bible. The love comes from the lessons you could learn from reading it. The hate comes from the misuse of it. You can use the bible to encourage others. And you can use the bible to hurt them as well. So use of the bible is a double edged sword. Referring back to the movie "The Book of Eli" Denzel Washington who plays Eli is a man with a mission to carry the last remaining copy of the bible to a safe place. Gary Oldman is trying to find a copy of the bible to use and control the minds of people. For the duration of the movie you see Denzel is using the bible for good reason while Gary is intent on using it for the wrong reasons.

How you approach reading the bible is important. When your intentions and motivations are clear you will likely have a better and more fulfilling journey in your readings. Regular and consistent reading of the bible helps open your mind to passages you probably wouldn't run into doing a search. As a Christian there is little excuse not to get into the bible.

If you truly want to enter into study there are a variety of ways. For example you have the text bible which is a regular bible. You have study bibles geared towards any age group. And if you don't feel like purchasing a bible you can go online to websites that carry numerous translations of the bible. There are bible apps and audio versions of the bible too. There may be a number of ways to get into the bible but the most important thing is actually reading and using it if you decide to get one. Possessing a bible is easy. Anyone can get a bible. However the question here is will your bible be something that is used and read, or simply another piece of furniture? Do not just be hearers of the word, be doers also (Jam. 1:22-24). A Collect in the Book of Common Prayer calls on us to read, mark, learn, and inwardly digest the word. Even Jesus makes a case for this: *"Blessed rather are those who hear the word of God and obey it"* (Lk. 11:28). Go and do likewise.

There was a movie called "Lost in Translation" starring Bill Murray playing an actor that goes to Japan to shoot a commercial. During the movie there is a scene where he is shooting a commercial and the director says a bunch of things to him in Japanese. The translator then walks over to Bill Murray and says barely one sentence to him. Bill then says what was probably what we were all thinking when he asks if that's all the director said, it seemed like more was said.

If you don't speak Hebrew, Greek, or Aramaic fluently you are likely going to be reading an English translation (or whatever language you are comfortable speaking). Whichever version you chose to read keep in mind a group of scholars sat down with numerous ancient texts to put together the bible sitting in your home and on store shelves. There are pros and cons to each version available so just make sure you select a fair choice when pursing to read and study the bible.

The King James Bible is one of the most enduring of the translations that have survived through the centuries. However it is not the first attempt at translation of texts or the last. For a time the only bible the church followed was the Latin Vulgate. Just as when Greek was the dominant language the Septuagint was made available for use. Septuagint was a Greek translation of Old Testament books which included later books that became known as the Apocrypha. When Latin became the dominant language Jerome was commissioned to translate the bible into Latin which resulted in the Latin Vulgate.

The first attempt of a translation of the bible into English was John Wycliffe's bible which appeared in 1382. Later to be followed by William Tyndale in 1520's. Tyndale's bible would have far reaching influences following the Reformation because later English translations would incorporate the translations of Tyndale into theirs. The translations that followed would be: Great Bible of 1539, Geneva Bible 1560, the Bishop's Bible of 1568, and the Douay–Rheims Bible of 1582-1609 finally getting to the King James in 1611.

If you are not sure how reliable the translation is, there are ways to check. First read the section addressed to the reader in the translation. That will explain how they assembled that translation. The approach of how that translation came about is briefly explained as well as their methods in its creation. The section addressed to the reader will usually appear in translations that are not public domain like the King James. Most translations after the King James Bible will likely have a copyright. Because the English language has changed a lot over the centuries there have been revisions to update the text to better match how we speak English today. And a translation never fully satisfies everyone so there will always be various versions available.

Also look at the footnotes at the bottom of the pages. They will tell you how the verses translated match the original text. The scholars at times might have struggled with the right way to word the text so the footnotes show what may have proved difficult with the translating. Also there may be notations where they guess at what the text is saying. However scholars who worked on the available translations have examined the numerous texts available to make the versions for use today. So the choice left for you now is which translation works best for your personal study.

The King James Bible has been around for years. The later versions that came out took advantage of the texts that were found which were older than the texts that were available when the scholars put together the King James Version. The later versions didn't just simply update the language of a King James Bible.

One time during Acolyte Practice I took out the Book of Common Prayer and along with an acolyte I was training we looked up Collects. There are two versions of Collects one is traditional and one is contemporary. Traditional sounds close to the wording of the King James Bible. And Contemporary sounds close to the way we speak today. She read the contemporary version with little difficulty. And I read traditional version. She had a hard time understanding what I read but I assured her we read the same thing. It was just worded differently. As we continue to learn and understand the various languages that currently exist and some that are no longer are used, certain things may be evaluated.

In reading commentaries about which bible translation is the best there was always the same conclusion. There are a number of good translations out there. But in the end it is recommended that you have at least two translations available for use so that if a text is not clear in one version the other one might be clearer. Also they mention two methods used in translation. One is dynamic equivalence and the other is formal equivalence. The advantage of a bible using dynamic equivalence is that you a have more readable/understandable translation. But the problem is the translator sometimes writes what they think the text means as opposed to what is actually said. The advantage of a bible using formal equivalence is that it minimizes the translator using their thoughts on the text. But the problem is that this usually results in a wooden translation that is not always readable or understandable. So choose a bible that is a good mix of both methods. Or pick bibles that make good use of each method to help balance out your study of the word.

There was a moment back in college when I was involved in a bible study group. We were reading Philippians. They were using New International Version while I was using New Revised Standard Version. Then it became my turn to read. The following is what I read: *"but emptied himself, taking the form of a slave, being born in human likeness. And being found in human form"* (Phil. 2:7). That is the verse as it appears in a New Revised Standard Version of the bible. It was a surprising after lifting my head up after reading to find the whole group staring at me. The New International Version is worded differently and what took them by surprise was when I said 'taking the form of a slave'. One of them said they found new meaning from the text because in the New International Version the text uses 'servant' instead of 'slave'. The study went off in a different direction and sparked an unexpected conversation. We eventually got back on track and finished our original discussion. The mood was similar to after Jesus read the scroll of Isaiah and following his reading all in the synagogue was looking at him. But unlike Jesus I didn't say the scripture was fulfilled.

Going back to an earlier comment about bibles mentioned in my possession. My church used a King James Bible for years. Then in the early 90's they switched to New Revised Standard Version with the Apocrypha. The New Revised Standard Version is a translation that boasts about being the most widely authorized by churches. Given that there are three editions of New Revised Standard Version bible available it is not hard to argue that point. There is the standard edition with or without the Apocrypha/Deuterocanonical books and there is the Roman Catholic Edition which has the "Apocrypha or Deuterocanonical books" in the order of the Latin Vulgate.

Most of you will likely have bibles that contain the Old and New Testaments that are part of the official canon. However depending on traditions established in your individual churches some might likely be using bibles without Apocrypha books. The Episcopal Church came out of the Catholic Church and bares certain similarities. So there are varying degrees of usage for Apocrypha books. They are not regularly used in daily readings but on some occasions they are used. Just know I will not be using any texts that are from the Apocryphal books here given that everyone probably does not have bibles with those books available.

This is not the part where I give you a song and dance about how great the New Revised Standard Version of the bible is. The New Revised Standard Version is considered a good translation however with a focus on gender neutral wording, the text falls away from the literal translation established by earlier translations. For example where the text in the New Testament reads as "brothers", it would read as: brothers and sisters, beloved, or believers. And some feel that the language is not as free flowing or a natural sounding English as it could be. There were a few times when quoting from New Revised Standard my grammar was corrected. Unless otherwise stated the biblical texts appearing in this book are as they appear in a New Revised Standard Version bible.

The New International Version bible is fairly popular because of its readability. Unlike the New Revised Standard Version the wording of an NIV is usually easier to follow. Recently the NIV went through a revision in 2011. I am not sure fully how the new revision will affect the popularity. When quoting from the NIV the texts that appear here are as they appear in the 2011 revision. I do not own a copy of the recent revision. But thanks to the power of the internet it was easy to access the revised version and match the texts used here.

If you are not sure which version you should use. Start with the one currently at your church. Or the bible that is currently in your home. Then branch off into reading a version that speaks the best to you. The most important thing about owning a bible is that you actually take time to read it. *"For whatever was written in former days was written for our instruction, so that by steadfastness and by encouragement of scriptures we might have hope"* (Rom. 15:4). If we are going to follow that message we must be able to adapt it to how we speak and talk today in order to maintain relevance. A balancing act must be done in this. First we must have ourselves rooted in the past to know where our beliefs and faith comes from. Then we need to grow and understand how to make what we do relatable to current situations. This means reading, studying, growth in understanding, and ultimately applying what we learn. That is how words truly have power. *"Heaven and earth will pass away, but my words will not pass away"* (Matt. 24:35).

CHAPTER THREE

Play to Your Own Strengths

"And the Spirit immediately drove him out into the wilderness" (Mk. 1:12).

This is where the journey begins. After following the lead in the first chapter "Calling", you have more than likely spent time eliminating any excuses as well as inadequacies you believed you had. Now that you have done away with the potential baggage that would have prevented you from doing what you had to do. Now comes the fun part which is evaluating your skills and resources. As well as developing your skills.

When you get called for something whether major or minor it is easy to feel inadequate or not up to it. However no matter what challenge or trial is set before you, do not quit too easily. It is real easy to duck and cower because you feel you are not ready for something. A lot may be asked and expected of you. If you feel you are not ready for something, take a moment. Evaluate what your strengths are and where you are lacking. Find out what is really needed of you. Then find a way to overcome those weaknesses.

When you watch some of the epic adventure movies out there a few common things are usually in place. You have a hero who is probably not equipped to save the day. The hero has to battle some issues before winning out in the end. The same could be said for some videogames. The character is not equipped to win. But over time the character gathers the necessary items, abilities, and experience to win in the end. Developing the tools, resources, strength among other things needed to succeed comes from going on a Wilderness journey.

Everyone on some level undergoes some trial or test. The more famous of tests is the Wilderness Test. When you are in Wilderness Test it is a usually a period of time where you develop the necessary skills needed to handle a situation. In churches that follow the Catholic tradition we commemorate the Wilderness journey of Jesus with the season of Lent. Lent is a period of fasting, praying, and to a degree reflection. Some people use that time to avoid some form of temptation. My approach to Lent in recent years has been to take an honest look at myself. What am I doing? What should be done more? How to get where I need to go? When you take an honest evaluation of your skills, you will know where you need help to become successful.

It is not necessarily a trip to the woods on a retreat. The test however takes place around the start of the call. It can also happen when you need to reevaluate things. You may feel inadequate for the task ahead. But this type of training will bring you full circle and help you realize you're potential.

Where you are lacking this is the place to work on those issues. Your world already got larger given the new responsibilities. Now it is up to you to strip away the old and remake yourself to do what needs to be done. This period depends on the situation. So be patient at this time. Transformations take time. Be strong and endure and things will turn out well.

There are various other tests that we face in our lives that help shape us to get where we need to go. One is the Time Test. This allows us to grow in faith. We all have a measure of trust and confidence. However this test allows us to purify our motives and attitudes. Whatever impure, proud and selfish motives exist will likely be removed through this test. Another test is the Character Test. This test shows areas of weakness in a person. Whatever hidden deficiencies still exist will be fleshed out here.

Great skill is shown after a price is paid in preparation for the opportunity. You do not choose timing of trials in your life. But you do choose to learn from them. It takes time and trials to grow as an individual and as a leader. And as people of faith it also takes God's help.

With that said the following stories coming from the bible will focus on specific areas needed to develop as an individual and as a leader. On that note using examples of biblical figures specific skills and attitudes will be on display. Interpersonal skills, good and bad advice, team building, maximizing your resources, as well as organizing and executing plans.

Take the story of Joseph in Genesis for example. He starts off as the favorite in the family. He is his father's favorite child. However he is at odds with his brothers right away. Before the bible states that he is a favorite child of his father Jacob. It makes note of him early on with his brothers being a bit of a tattletale. While shepherding the flock with his brothers he brings a bad report about them to his father (Gen. 37:2).

Then he has two dreams where he appears above his brothers only to bring more resentment (Gen. 37:5-11). Aspiring to greatness is not a bad thing. But if you lack respect and are at odds with people. You clearly will not go anywhere. Joseph lacked interpersonal skills. And he was at odds with his family. This is where his wilderness journey began.

What could possibly be a doomed situation ended up being a journey that empowered Joseph. At first his brothers plotted to kill him, only to end up selling Joseph into slavery (Gen. 37:18-28). He ended up being bought by an officer of Pharaoh named Potiphar who was captain of the guard.

Despite the situation the bible states that God was with Joseph and that he became a successful man in the house of his master. Over time his master realized that God was with Joseph and that everything prospered in his hands. Joseph was then made overseer of the house and put in charge of everything (Gen. 39:2-6). However this was not the end of the story. Joseph was sold into slavery as a teenager and grew successful as well as handsome. He ran into trouble with the wife of his master and ended up in prison. Even in prison the bible states that God was with Joseph (Gen. 39:21). While in prison he helped two people interpret their dreams. He helped them with hopes that he would be freed from prison. But upon their release they did not remember Joseph.

However when the Pharaoh needed help interpreting his dreams Joseph was then remembered and helped out the Pharaoh. Not only did he help the Pharaoh interpret the dream he helped form a plan on how to deal with it. Joseph at age thirty was then put into service of the Pharaoh second only to the Pharaoh (Gen. 41:1-46). Joseph may not have known how to deal with people beforehand. But after all the trials he went through from years of slavery and prison set the stage for the success he eventually achieved in life.

Following the lead from the story of Joseph you see a gradual development of people skills. He started off at being at odds with his family. After being sold into slavery he then was able to work with others while managing the affairs of a household. This made helping to lead the affairs of a nation easier.

Joseph was destined to do well and be successful as a leader and as a person. However he needed to be conditioned to shoulder such a task. Whatever skills he lacked was likely honed during his time as a slave. Do not be discouraged by an odd turn of events. They can still work out in your favor. Patience is important. Maintain a level of humility and things will come your way.

While searching for direction it is a good idea to get the best advice possible before starting out, as well as during your journey. *"Listen to advice and accept instruction, that you may gain wisdom for the future"* (Prov. 19:20). Mentors and advisors are valuable to leaders. There will always be a call for leaders. However there is also a need to help establish leaders as well. Where would Moses be without Jethro? (Ex. 18:13-26)

Where would Samuel be without advice from Eli? (1 Sam. 3:4-11) Where would Elisha be without Elijah? (1 Kings 19:19-21) Where would Hezekiah be without Isaiah? (2 Kings 19:5-7) Where would Josiah be without Huldah? (2 Kings 22:14-20) Where would Paul be without Ananias? (Acts 9:8-19) Whether it is advice or a spark to pave the way someone had a hand in something. Things do not happen without help. Moses will be discussed shortly. Hezekiah, Josiah and Paul will be discussed in the next chapter.

Staying on the subject for a bit when it comes to mentors and advisors, they can come at any point in your life whether it is the beginning, middle, or even at the end of a situation. I will share two stories involving my relationship with my protégé. One involves helping him find a topic for a sermon. The other involves improving how he delivered one.

The first story will deal with the sermon he performed in church the famous "Don't worry" sermon. This is the same sermon I touched on in the previous chapter. That sermon almost did not happen. The Sunday before he was tapped to speak he came to me for advice because he did not know what to do. He spoke before but given the activity surrounding him it was not easy to come up with ideas. I took out the church bulletin and we looked at the readings for next week. We started with the Gospel reading for that Sunday which was Matthew 6:25-34.

We read it and before I commented, I waited for his reaction. At first he was not sure what use if any there was with the reading. I then said never mind the text and focus on the topic. The topic was "Don't worry". The conversation went on to mean owning the topic in relation to what he deals with on a daily basis. When he grasped that suggestion it opened the door to him coming up with ideas on what he could say. He asked if he could use stories. My response was it was your show. If the stories help go for it. The uneasiness and concern made way to relief and most certainly confidence. He went on to give a powerful and emotionally charged sermon. It was one of the most talked about ones done for awhile.

Another situation was a sermon where the priest at the time added a few things for him to talk about. Knowing him the way I do it was easy to tell something was up when he was speaking during his sermon. There were moments where he seemed natural and at home with what he was talking about. And then there were moments where he seemed caught off guard by what he was talking about as he read certain parts of it.

After sermon I spoke to him about it. My question was how much of that did he write. And he said 60%. My response was I had a feeling that you did not write all of it, because some parts you seemed a bit off. So he gave a better reading of what was written before speaking again and it came out more naturally.

There is a level of trust between myself and my protégé. So he knows when I am speaking to him it is from a level of respect. And despite the age gap he knows it is not my intention to talk down to him. When giving advice you need to speak in a way that does not insult anyone's intelligence. That means the mentor and protégé need to have a decent level of communication. If you are not careful about how you speak to someone you can alienate them. And they will tune out any message you were trying to relate to them. When picking a mentor check that they are telling you what you need to hear for success. There are some that will tell you just what you want to hear and make you feel it is the right thing to do when it is all wrong. Exercise good judgment in this situation.

Here is an example of bad advice. Rehoboam stands out as an example of someone who took poor advice when assuming a leadership position. Rehoboam succeeded Solomon as king. As soon as he took power the assembly of Israel came to him. They stated that King Solomon laid heavy burdens on them and if he relieved it they would follow him (1 Kings 12:4). Rehoboam took a moment before answering them. He asked them to give him three days then while he sought advice on the matter.

To understand what the people were going through we need to look at the times of King Solomon. Unlike King Saul and King David the times of King Solomon were a time of peace. After King Solomon took the throne he set in motion plans to build the temple. He also built other things including his house. At times the building projects were done with forced labor (1 Kings 5:13, 1 Kings 9:15). The extent of the building projects are detailed in 1 Kings chapters 5-7. He built a spectacular temple and palace as well as modernized the army. Many riches were attained by Solomon at this time as well (1 Kings 10:14-29). Life was good. But the work put on the people to build wore on them.

Let us get back to Rehoboam. He was given two sets of advice. When he took counsel from the older men who served his father Solomon they told him if you do good for them they will follow you (1 Kings 12:7). But Rehoboam ignored the advice. Then he took counsel with the young men who grew up with him. And they gave him bad advice leading Rehoboam to promise to make the burdens harsher than it was with his father (1 Kings 12:10, 11). Following the bad advice from his friends, the people realized the king was not going to listen to them and the kingdom became split because of it.

Rehoboam was initially given the benefit of the doubt when he became king. All he had to do was work with the people but he did not. Leadership is not just about establishing rules and laws. It is about working with others as best you can. Be accommodating to others but do it with limits. Things need to get done however everyone needs to have a level of humility when it comes to working with each other. Listen to each other's needs. And most importantly compromise.

On the heels of bad advice here is an example of good advice. It involves the story of Moses and Jethro: *Moses' father-in-law said to him, "What you are doing is not good. You will surely wear yourself out, both you and these people with you. For the task is too heavy for you; you cannot do it alone"* (Ex. 18:17-18). This verse was used during a conversation I held about Team Building during Acolyte Practice. My initial comment was that the chapter is a story told in two halves. The first half has Moses being commended by his father-in-law Jethro following his successes. The second half features Jethro going what are you thinking?

Prior to the events laid out in Exodus chapter 18 you find during parts of the journey Moses was doing everything himself. People were hungry, Moses did something about it. People were thirsty, Moses did something about it. By the time you get to chapter 17 you are probably saying something has got to give. Near the end of that chapter there was a battle between the Israelites and Amalek (Ex. 17:8-13). When getting ready for the battle with Amalek, Moses said to Joshua to take some men and go into battle.

During the battle Moses stood a distance away and whenever he held up his hand the Israelites were successful. But when he lowered his hand the Amalek were successful. Eventually Aaron and Hur found a place for Moses to sit and the two held up Moses' hands until Joshua defeated Amalek. Moses clearly needed help. And the thing to notice here is being a good leader is one thing. But you need help and support as well to get things accomplished.

In getting back to Exodus chapter 18 Jethro noticed that everyone was coming to see Moses for everything. How many people were with Moses at this time? We don't really know. According to Exodus 12:37 there were 600,000 men. The first census was taken in the book of Numbers. And that was to establish a fighting force which in total was 603,550 (Num. 1:46). This however does not count women and children or even the elderly. Let us not forget that a group was set aside for worship purposes.

Jethro's parting advice to Moses was how to divide up the work. Moses retains his position as leader. However he should designate people to handle groups of people and entrust them with specific responsibilities. This will free up Moses to focus on bigger tasks without having to worry about every detail which creates more work than he needs to deal with.

This is also echoed in Deuteronomy 1:9-18. It leaves out the encounter with Jethro. But it explains how Moses addressed the crowd in terms of how he would divide up leadership responsibilities. Leaders were chosen and designated to handle groups of people. Moses was still the overall leader but he did not have to deal with every single person while figuring out the next move. And one person trying to manage thousands of people is an extremely tall order.

The discussion of Moses and Jethro led to recent experiences. In relating the verse to real life situations I gave examples. The first example was the trip to Washington National Cathedral for the National Acolyte Festival. The annual event invites Acolytes from various churches and denominations from across the country.

The event draws a capacity crowd which is around 3,000. One of the highlights of the event is the March of Acolytes. The various groups of Acolytes are marshaled (guided) by the Cathedral Vergers to march down the main aisle. This takes approximately 40 minutes. The rest of the service is straightforward. Communion goes by rather fast due to the communion stations setup to handle the crowds.

The goal was to explain to how dividing up the work the right way helps speed things along. Because the work was divided up by groups of people properly it didn't take all day for things to get done. If the Vergers were not on hand directing traffic the March of Acolytes would probably have been sloppy and chaotic. But the team of Vergers managed the crowds and things were done orderly and decent. If they did not use Communion stations to divide up the distribution of communion that would lead to longer lines that can take long to finish. No matter how great or small the task. Make sure you understand how to organize and divide up the work.

There was a difference with the situations involving Rehoboam and Moses. The tone of the voices varies here. However in the case of Rehoboam he got two sets of advice. One was from the group of old men who suggested what he needed to hear in order to lead his people. The other was from a group of young men who told him what he wanted to hear. In the end what he followed was the advice he wanted to hear and it ended badly.

In the case of Moses, his father-in-law pointed out what Moses was doing wrong. The advice given ultimately helped Moses. Sometimes advisors will be either kind or to some extent firm. In the end it is just advice. It is up to you what you do with the information. The success and failure is on you. So whatever you choose to do make sure it is something that is a benefit to all and helps others in need at the time out. On the heels of that let us look at Gideon making the most of his resources.

Concerning Gideon his call to lead came when the Midianites were oppressing the Israelites. They would attack and take away produce and livestock making it almost impossible to survive in the land. *"Thus Israel was greatly impoverished because of the Midian; and the Israelites cried out to the LORD for help"* (Judg. 6:6).

Gideon is known for lacking confidence at the beginning of his call. When God told him to destroy the altar of Baal, Gideon did it in secret at a time no one would notice (Judg. 6:25-27). He asked several times for proof that God was with him (Judg. 6:36-40). So it was rather interesting what happened when the army assembled for Gideon to lead. When the troops assembled God told Gideon there were too many to fight the Midianites with. *The LORD said to Gideon, "The troops with you are too many for me to give the Midianites into their hand. Israel would only take the credit away from me, saying, 'My own hand has delivered me'* (Judg. 7:2).

Over the time the thousands of troops were gradually cut down to 300 men. This is a fraction of what Moses had when wandering with the Israelites during the Exodus. However despite the small number Gideon was about to make it work. God told Gideon if he feared attacking the camp of Midian spy on the group and then he would find the strength to do it (Judg. 7:9-11). Afterwards Gideon divided up his troops and gave them instructions on how to attack (Judg. 7:16-22). The attack confused and defeated the enemy. Gideon then went on to successfully liberate his people afterwards. Despite a small group of people working with him, Gideon managed to do what was needed. Be patient with what you have. Then gradually figure out the best way to make the most of what you have. Ideally you want a certain amount but it may not be in the cards. However with determination and courage you will get where you need to go. Also be persistent.

The story of Nehemiah takes place during the Persian period. The Babylonian invasion signaled the fall of the Israelites. *"They burned the house of God, broke down the wall of Jerusalem, burned all its palaces with fire, and destroyed all its precious vessels"* (2 Chr. 36:19). Then Jerusalem was left in a fractured state after the invasion. And groups of people were sent into exile and became servants.

However Babylon was later conquered by the Persians. And under the rule of King Cyrus of Persia, the Israelites were allowed to return home to Jerusalem. *"Thus says King Cyrus of Persia: The LORD, the God of heaven, has given me all the kingdoms of the earth, and he has charged me to build him a house at Jerusalem, which is in Judah. Whoever is among you of all his people, may the LORD his God be with him! Let him go up"* (2 Chr. 36:23). For better details on the fall of Jerusalem see 2 Kings 25.

Nehemiah hears the situation about the problems facing the Israelites in Jerusalem. One of Nehemiah's brothers gave him this news about the Jews who escaped captivity and was in Jerusalem: *They replied, "The survivors there in the province who escaped captivity are in great trouble and shame; the wall of Jerusalem is broken down, and its gates have been destroyed by fire"* (Neh. 1:3).

The wall was a big deal especially in those times. The walls meant security and you were able to defend your homes easier. If you saw movies where invading forces attacked a structure, you probably noticed that as long as the wall remained intact they could hold off the attackers. But it was after the walls were breached that chaos resulted. The people were vulnerable to attack. So a need to restore the wall to protect them was needed.

Nehemiah went through a period of mourning, fasting and praying hoping to find a solution to the problem (Neh. 1:4-11). Afterwards he went to the king and asked for help. Nehemiah was probably hesitant to ask for help at first, because the king noticed Nehemiah's uneasiness. Nehemiah took a moment and then told the king what was bothering him. After this the king then asked how long Nehemiah how long it might take. This led to Nehemiah setting a date (Neh. 2:1-6).

After the date was set Nehemiah requested letters that provided him passage to Judah. And a letter that helped him get supplies needed to build with. The king granted all that Nehemiah requested for the journey and the rebuilding projects (Neh. 2:7, 8). Nehemiah spent three days in Jerusalem. He did not tell anyone what he was up to. And he spent the night inspecting the damage to the areas (Neh. 2:11-16). Afterwards Nehemiah makes it public what his intentions are for being there. He is there to help rebuild the wall. The rest of the story is summarized as follows. He explains the need to rebuild (Neh. 2:17, 18). The seeds of opposition to rebuild the wall take shape. But they are thwarted (Neh. 4:1-20). Mission is accomplished and the rebuilding is complete (Neh. 6:15, 16).

Nehemiah had to have good people skills to get things done. He had an idea of what he needed to do. He had a plan to rebuild. And he had to express his grand plan in a way that others could follow it. So have a plan but make sure people get where you are coming from this way there won't be questions and follow up questions to a plan you think is easy. Simplification is important here. Slight correction there may still be questions. But you won't spend too long answering and explaining things.

He needed to include as many people as possible and move forward with those who were ready. He organized groups of people to take on sections to work on. This is a combination of cooperation, participation and delegation. And because of the surrounding opposition he had to organize workers and defense of each other as well. That is where preparation comes into play. And after you accomplish your goals it is important to celebrate any and all achievements.

During a television interview former Hockey player Mark Messier was asked what made him a good leader. He started out by quoting Abraham Lincoln: "No man is good enough to govern another man without that others consent." He then went on to discuss that you need to develop trust and honesty with people. Developing skills as a leadership is an ongoing process. However if people cannot trust or believe in you, success will be minimal if at all.

Honesty is another valuable asset in working with a group. You need to be honest with those you deal with. Another part of honest is integrity. Once you compromise your integrity it is lost. Integrity is considered an admirable trait. Therefore you must keep yourself honest above all else in your dealings with others.

You need to have a visionary outlook. Have a vision and a focus as to where you want to go. See where you are. See where you want to go. And then figure out how you can get there. Being able to do that takes effort.

You need to be a good team builder to help you get where you need to go for success. When looking at the example of Moses it looks like it took awhile before he organized the large group following him. Teaching groups of people to govern themselves takes time and patience. When Jesus selected twelve disciples as recorded in Luke, it states he spent all night in prayer (Lk. 6:12). Even after that when the story shifts to him instructing them things did not look promising. After selecting your team you have to organize them to help you achieve your goals. Following the announcement by Nehemiah to rebuild the wall, the entire chapter 3 of Nehemiah discusses how the work was organized and how duties and responsibilities were given out.

Team building starts with you. Take an honest look at yourself. What your strengths and weaknesses are. While running a group, make sure the people surrounding you compliment what you are trying to do. In recognizing your weaknesses make sure there are people to supplement where you are lacking. Along with improving your situation, make sure the structure allows you to get where you need to go without burning yourself. Spread out the work so you avoid sweating minor details that can be easily handled by someone else. You still have to put the work in. Just make sure that the ones supporting you know what to do. Again communication is important.

Keep your ego in check. A lot may be asked or expected of you in a given time. But with patience things will work out. Recognize first how long you will be involved with a group of people. If it is a short term situation being overtly technical is pointless. Just focus on getting from point A to point B as best as you can. If it is long term situation then gradually take steps to tweak things so it is closer to where you would like to go. And keep track of what you are doing so you do not constantly reinvent the wheel every time. If it went well the first time there is no need to change it again and again. Just improve on what you did.

Be mindful of how you talk to people. Initially you do not know how to talk to someone. But when you take a moment to find out who you are dealing with that can develop into a comfortable level of communication. We are individuals. We may be created the equally. But our mindsets, viewpoints and attitudes vary. When people have a mutual understanding then it is less likely anyone will be offended easily. You can say something that insults someone's intelligence. The problem is that most of the time it is done unintentionally. So be on guard about that. Again the better a group knows each other the less possibility there will be friction.

Be careful how you judge the people you are dealing with. *"Do not judge by appearances, but judge with right judgment"* (Jn. 7:24). It all goes back to calling. The value of a person may not be there initially but in time you will see it. The more you work with people the better you will get to know them. When planning out things have a structure in place to fall back on. *For which of you, intending to build a tower, does not first sit down and estimate the cost, to see whether he has enough to complete it? Otherwise, when he has laid a foundation and is not able to finish, all who see it will begin to ridicule him, saying, 'This fellow began to build and was not able to finish'* (Lk. 14:28-30).

As a leader and an individual you will have plans and goals you want accomplished. Just remember the outcome depends on what you reap. Low expectations bring low results. Just as high expectations will yield better results. After you took an honest look at whom you are as a person. You can structure your team better to get where you need to go. This means being able to work with others to get things done.

A leader sees farther than others see. More than others see. And you see before others see. Leaders not only know where they are going they also know how to get there. Leaders also know how to take people with them. Leaders find purpose in the needs around them.

Your mission is the focus of your priorities. See the whole picture then decide what needs to be focused on. When needs comes up step back, and look at the big picture. Then determine the appropriate action according to your priorities. Focus on a few things and trust others to do the rest. Spend time on what needs to be done. Give your best time to your most important tasks.

It is admirable to be ambitious and hardworking, it is better to be smart working. Being efficient is not about checking all items off the to-do list. It is in forming a habit of prioritizing your time so you focus on what is important. Leaders put first things first. Leaders see everything but focus on important things. Leaders invest their time in what produces the greatest return. Leaders position people where everybody wins.

When my current Rector came to church I gave him a card with the following verse: *"Know well the condition of your flocks, and give attention to your herds"* (Prov. 27:23). A leadership position does not mean you "impose your will" on someone or a group of people. Jesus himself says the greatest will be a servant in Matthew 23:11. So check your ego at the door and maintain a level of humility in performing your duties.

When dealing with a group of people work on good communication skills. The better people know where you are coming from the easier it will be handing out assignments. And you create less work for yourself having to check what others are doing. Shooting for the moon is ok but make sure the people coming along for the ride can execute the plan. Otherwise it is doomed to fail.

Again communication is important to be a great leader. The reason is simple: you can have other great qualities to be a leader. But if you fail to communicate you will never be effective as a leader. A good communicator can connect with others to move the group forward.

Good communication develops good relationships. Failure to establish good relationships means poor leadership skills and poor skills as a team player. Bottom line is you need to be able to equip yourself with good communication skills and learn ways to relate your ideas to others.

As stated before I am the Verger at my church. My situation is unique because I am the first person to ever hold that title here. The good thing about being first means you are entering a situation without baggage from predecessors. The bad thing is getting advice on the right way to apply things associated with your ministry is at times difficult. That is because there is no one around to tell you how to approach things the right way. Educate yourself, while educating others.

Thankfully I am a member of the Vergers Guild of the Episcopal Church. So with that said I am never truly alone in figuring out what to do. And along with advice there are others available to give a helping hand. When I started to get involved in services at cathedrals it was an eye opening experience. There is nothing like being involved in services at a cathedral. No matter how large a crowd the church attracts it is usually dwarfed by the capacity of a cathedral. Being involved in services there helped me better understand how to work within a group setting involving Vergers. Seeing how they plan events helped me take notes on how to incorporate a simplified version of the cathedral on a church level. I was never trained as a Verger however involvement in activities elsewhere like cathedrals and other churches helped me out. No one trained me. I trained myself.

I noticed that when it came to planning events at the cathedral. Occasionally there have been invitations to assist with services at the Cathedral of St. John the Divine. The Head Verger (or the one designated to coordinate us) at the cathedral left the more basic routines to the additional Vergers. While the Head Verger focused on the potentially complicated things. This means that when it came to the more critical areas of the worship service. The Head Verger was likely better focused on certain details because he did not burn out sweating minor stuff that anyone else could have possibly handled. In the end while involved in major events at the cathedral and taking notes on how things were planned. It became easier to deal with and manage planning and organizing the groups of Acolytes and Vergers surrounding me during events. At my church I am both the Head Verger and the Acolyte Director so managing two ministries becomes interesting in a given situation. I fused the ministries into one title calling myself the Acolyte Verger. Vergers involved in more than one ministry have fused titles as well. So this is not a new thing.

Before launching into a series of stories involving me and what we discussed I need to update events a bit. The first chapter was concluded with my journey to becoming Verger at my church. The following stories take place a few years later. There was a transition period where my former Rector left in July 2010 and a new one came in December 2012. Vergers are not clergy so I did not need to hand in resignation letters to the priest. However Vergers in the church are appointed by the Rector or recognized Head Priest of the church. So if the new Rector does not recognize the appointment of a Verger, it is done. The Rector can fire me as Verger but I was not fired. Upon arrival one of his first meetings was with the Acolytes. The Acolytes are the busiest of the groups that assist him so it was important that we are on the same page with him. He asked who the Master of Ceremonies (MC) at the church was.

The closest we have to a Master of Ceremonies is the head of the Acolytes which is me. The Rector empowers the MC to carry out what he needs done during services. Unfortunately given the activity surrounding me I waved off that responsibility. He needed someone who was going to be a mainstay standing around him and I move around a lot taking care of things. Someone else was given that responsibility. I still focused on handling organizing activity and responsibility of the Acolytes and any Vergers that were with me on a given day. Instead of simply planning duties and informing the priest of what was going on. I now give that information to the designated person so they know what was going on.

Now I am going to share two stories that come to mind in relation to what we are discussing here. Both events surround my involvement in the church as Verger. The first one is the service involving the Installation of my current Rector in June 2013. As stated before, time went on I learned a few things to add to what I already knew about the order of service in the church. Being involved in services at other churches let alone at cathedrals expanded my wealth of knowledge. It was the equivalent of the story I shared with you in the first chapter involving Dr. Ben Carson when it came to discussing getting experience. The trip gave him a wealth of knowledge.

Going into the preparation for the Installation Service I remembered the atmosphere when my former priest was installed as Rector in 1991. Most notably part of what my predecessor who ran the Acolytes at the time went through. He was constantly being given directions on what to do and how to plan out during the service. Years later I would be in his shoes knowing I would go through the same thing.

However the ministry of Vergers was not established in the church at the time my predecessor ran the Acolytes. That would take place in 2006. So in my case there were more tools at my disposal. My church is dubbed the Cathedral of the Bronx. It took a step forward in that regard when the Verger ministry was added to the church. The experience and knowledge gained during this time made dealing with whatever pressures came with this service easy. And after dealing with the Consecration and later Installation services for my current Bishop at the Cathedral of St. John the Divine confidence in being able to handle the upcoming situation became easier to bear.

Before I go into the events of my Rector's service I will discuss the events of the Consecration and Installation of the Bishop of the Diocese of N.Y. at the Cathedral of St. John the Divine. The planning for both had a similar feel. Prior to the Consecration Service and later on the Installation Service we had rehearsals. The Consecration Service was necessary because the Bishop Coadjutor elected was a priest and had to be consecrated as a Bishop. After a period of time when the

Bishop of the Diocese of N.Y. retired the Bishop Coadjutor would then be installed as the new Bishop. This is similar to the President Elect taking over when the outgoing President's term expires. The Installation Service was a passing of torch from the former Bishop to the current one. Think Elijah leaving Elisha in 2 Kings 2:9-12.

When at the cathedral for rehearsals the Master of Ceremonies along with the Head Verger and the Head of the Acolytes go over planning of the service. Members of the Usher board are sometimes present as well. At the cathedral the main duties of the Acolytes is the processions. However the Vergers are fairly active before, during, and after the service. So the longest meeting is usually with the Vergers. If the opening procession is complicated the Head Verger along with the Master of Ceremonies goes over the choreography of that. The rest is straightforward and all they are doing is figuring out who among the Vergers assembled will handle which situations. We usually get an assignment sheet so we know how the planning for the service is mapped out. Then on additional sheets we find out what other duties would need to be handled and who is responsible for that. When I am planning out the services that will include additional Vergers at my church, I would borrow from the planning at the cathedral and map out is needed from the group.

Getting back to the cathedral, after planning things out it is discussed and afterwards we move on. Long story short after the plan is discussed it is not game over. The heads of the individual ministries would then discuss with their groups how to handle planning their parts in the service. The groups would meet up before service to go over any other changes beforehand. Given that church activities are a volunteer service we need to keep in mind that people still have to deal with their regular jobs, family activities, and for some school activities among other situations. Perfect attendance at rehearsals is unlikely. But those who plan on being involved notify the heads of the groups ahead of time as to whether or not they will participate. That makes planning duties easier.

In preparation of the Installation Service for my Rector I had background information beforehand. Along with my former Rector's ceremony I was involved in four other Installation Services as a Verger. I was invited to a fellow Verger's church for the installation of his priest shortly after I was installed as Verger in 2006. In that service my main involvement was in the procession.

Two more came after my involvement in the farewell services for the former Vicar Bishop of my diocese in 2009 (they held a service at the Cathedral earlier and then on his last Sunday he was at my church). After the service held at the cathedral I took the format of how they organized Vergers at the cathedral for service and did a simplified version of it at church. The format I used to organize Vergers at the service for the Bishop ended up being the blueprint for how to use multiple Vergers in a service when heading into the next few services both at church and elsewhere. Someone saw how I organized Acolytes and Vergers at that service.

That service led to me being invited to a church locally for another Priest Installation. After a conversation with the priest I brought in a team of vergers to help me out. Near the end of that service a priest saw what we did and asked for our help. Then recently when the Chaplain of the Vergers Guild was being installed at his church, I was also in attendance. That was the only installation service where I was just present and not involved. But being a spectator I did observe and take note of things. You never know when something you see will come in handy somewhere else. Like a Priest I can be invited to serve at other events. However the Priest or Warden needs to be notified of my involvement in any events since I represent their church.

I was a kid when it came to my former Rector's Installation Service. Thankfully I did not have to rely on what I remembered from a good twenty years ago. Given recent involvement in Installation Services for Priests it was easier to figure out what probably would go on. This also made setting up a structure to work in real easy as well. The goal prior to rehearsals was not to solve all the planning. It was to spread out as much responsibility as possible. And leave room for myself to react to things that may or may not have been planned. Both groups have a level of trust in me as a group leader so it wasn't hard planning Verger and Acolyte routines. Again I was both Head Verger and Head of the Acolytes. So anyone affiliated with those ministries fell under my leadership at my church.

The Installation Service varies depending on what the priest wants to do that day. There is a format and the priest can either go with what is set or add to it. I had to wait until the day of rehearsals to find out the planning. But in the meantime assembling the team was important. After the date was set for the service, I put out a call to the Vergers that assisted me at a previous service that said they wanted to be involved with this one. After finding out how many Acolytes and Vergers were possibly coming, the next steps in planning would get easier. Setting up a meeting to go over possible areas was established.

A curve ball was thrown into the mix because the month of May is a busy month with holidays and events. So I ended up just meeting with the Vergers that were coming for the event. Right away I stated that most of what we discuss is a guess since it was not clear what is fully being planned that day. However Vergers can be slipped into any situation without disrupting what is going on. As a Verger or an Acolyte your bread and butter is the order of service. So having a working knowledge of the upcoming service makes it easier to assist the Clergy in planning. My goal with the team of Vergers was naturally to have a structure in place so that when the planning became more evident for the service there would be less scrambling that day. And less time spent on last minute planning. The group has seen my church stuffed. But they have never seen overflow. Getting them comfortable with what may happen will mean fewer hassles for me.

In the picture provided there were three Vergers alongside me. Two out of three have been alongside me for Priest Installations. While one is a fellow Verger I worked alongside with at the Cathedral of St. John the Divine. Collectively we have seen the event enough times to guess at possible trouble areas of the service. We started with the basic ceremonial duties that would likely be expected from us. First I discussed the Cross procession at the beginning of the service. There was a three cross procession. And the Bishop was last in the procession. When the bulletin for the service was setup, Vergers were not listed in the procession. However Vergers were listed in the bulletin. I handled giving out all assignments to them. There were four Vergers involved in the service. Three took care of leading the three crosses. And one would lead the Bishop. On a side note the incoming Priest was from the Diocese of Long Island so as a hidden joke I posted a Verger from that Diocese to lead that cross.

Next came assigning Vergers to escort the readers. There were two readers that day. Knowing I would likely be running around a lot. It became important to limit how much ceremonial duties I performed that day. After assigning who escorted the readers, I lead the sermon. Looking back on how the cathedral did communion stations and thinking of overflow we discussed dealing with stations. At the cathedral the Vergers moved those assigned to distribute communion to their stations. Given how slow the movement was to get to communion stations the last couple of times at church during big events. It felt necessary that in this situation to have Vergers move people to their places as soon as possible.

I showed the Vergers where the stations would likely be in the rear of the church and downstairs for the overflow crowd. As well as assigned who handled them. I would be roaming making sure no one ran out of anything. The meeting was a healthy one. And I encouraged questions since there is a chance of possibly missing something. You can guess and project a lot of things. But unless you hear any actual planning all you are doing is guessing and hoping that it works. We moved about walking and talking about possible trouble areas. Afterwards we went out to eat. This was a further bonding of the team.

Following that I drew up a plan of what was discussed at the meeting and handed it over to the wardens who oversaw planning of the service as well as one of the MC's for the service. There were two of them. One from the church and the other is a Priest from another church. Indirectly I was also a MC but unlike the established ones I would be more active in the service.

Before the rehearsals I joked that no matter how it was dressed the service would fall squarely on my shoulders. And ultimately it did. During rehearsals the established Master of Ceremonies (MC) clearly wanted to have me doing all the running that day. It was the typical have the guy that knows everything do the entire work situation. The person instead of making the most of all his resources decided to just burn out one person.

Instead of finding out first who was going to be at the service and what people had a talent for. He decided to plan on the fly with whoever was there that day. That set the tone for a lot of friction. Not all acolytes were present that day. Some were still in class, while others were at events. Just like at the cathedral not everyone made the rehearsals. So as long as there was an idea of who was coming planning was made with the expectation of others coming. Details can easily be explained the day of the service as long as the plan was known beforehand. Aside from the processions there was not much difference from what the groups normally do. And I can explain to anyone that was missing what they needed to do specifically prior to the service. After discussing the procession, the MC had me moving kneelers for the Priest to kneel before the Sanctuary. As well as move around the old Bishop's chair which has not seen use in decades. It was a huge chair by the way. Move things into place and then move them out of the way.

All of this was done before the Readers. And the MC wanted me to lead the readers too. A slight argument started because it was clear I was doing too much early on. And the only thing going on was assigning me every possible duty during the service. I stuck to my guns and left the assignments as I planned it. For the record what I planned turned out well. Glad I passed the basic assignments on to other Vergers because it freed me up for any hiccups that might occur in the service. Especially since some details were not covered during rehearsals.

After seeing the plan for the service that was when I went to work. As Head Verger and Head Acolyte it was up to me to make sure members of both groups knew what they were doing. Before leaving church that night I sat and looked at the Order of Procession and picked it apart. First began placing the Vergers in the procession. That part was easy since I knew how many were going to be there. Then wrote a list of Acolytes I knew were likely coming that day and wrote what assignments they would have during the service. When I got home I looked at the order of service and worked from memory on what may or may not be covered and plugged as many holes that there might be in the planning of the service.

The gift giving part if not approached right could take all day. And potentially be messy. During the ceremony the Priest is presented with gifts welcoming them to the church. That can be grand or simple.

Thankfully the focus was mainly on the church groups. The rest gave gifts at a later date. The big question is where to put the gifts gathered. When asking the MC about it he needed a moment. Then he said get a table. I ended up grabbing a small table and placing it in an area that was easy to get to. When the time came and the Priest was presented with gifts it was easy to place them somewhere and keep the service going. The rest of the service was easy going for the most part. Despite the lack of collaboration things went well. In the end whatever planning I did made the difference leading to the success of the service.

The next story involves the planning for the 100th Anniversary celebration of our church during the weeklong celebration. This was in October of the same year. Sunday would combine crowds from both services in one service that morning with a big luncheon to follow. There would be four days of Revival Services. Revival Services do not require much activity from me aside from setting the readings as well as lighting and extinguishing candles. The main event was on St. Luke's Day which is October 18 and was a Friday that year. That night would feature a visit from our Bishop. After getting a look at the plan following rehearsals it became easier to organize the Acolytes and Vergers. The focus will be on the events of St. Luke's Day.

Rehearsals were done the day before the weeklong celebration. During the Installation Service it was a priest from another church who did the bulk of the planning along with someone who knew me. This time the Master of Ceremonies was just someone from the church who knew me. So when it came time to planning how to deal with the events there was less friction. The service for Sunday was straightforward. But because the priest combined rehearsals for both Sunday morning and Friday night people were a bit confused. There would be a grand procession which included a collection of banners representing all the groups in the church. It was thought of that the banners would only be used for St. Luke's Day, but it turns out that the banners would also be used for Sunday morning. The services for both days were straightforward. And there was not much that needed tweaking going into that week. There was a problem area that I ended up going over with a fellow verger after rehearsals.

The problem was mainly dealing with the procession to the Baptismal Font. During the service was a Renewal of Baptismal Vows. At that time the water is blessed for use followed by the blessing of the crowd with the water. The procession takes an L shape march up the aisle to the font. However the return trip back is fine if all you are doing is heading back to your seats. If the Bishop is going to bless the crowd he would need to circle the church once and then go down the aisle to get everyone. I discussed it with the Master of Ceremonies and they said talk to the priest. So I talked it over with the priest and he agreed. Since there were going to be multiple Vergers there it would be easy to place a Verger in front the Bishop to follow while everyone else went to their seats.

I must add that the entire altar party was heading to the font that night. So Acolytes, Altar Servers, Eucharistic Ministers/ Visitors, and Visiting Clergy were in the procession. It was not clear how much Visiting Clergy was coming. Which means it could be more crowded than planned. Another question was who was the Cantor for that night if they were not using a Deacon? And would that person know when to start reading? Lastly later on there was supposed to be a special collection for the anniversary service. How were they going to handle moving around the container for collection?

In dealing with these open questions that is when I got started resolving them. Offhand the only number I couldn't approximate that night was the number of Visiting Clergy. That is never an exact number beforehand. But since I had a team of Vergers coming that night it was easy to have a Verger in front the cross leading the procession who would at the right time marshal the crowd so that there would be a easy path for the Priest and the Bishop heading to the font. People in the procession to the font would likely bunch up clogging the passage way making it hard for others to get where they needed to go. With that said assigning a Verger to direct traffic was a must.

The other assignments were easy to plan out. The two readers were the Wardens so Vergers were assigned to escort them. Along with having Vergers escort the readers the plan was to have one lead the Bishop to the pulpit for the sermon. With that said the same Verger can lead the Bishop to the Baptismal Font, and then around the church blessing the crowd with water. The Cantor was a member of the Choir so a Verger was assigned to escort that person. Not sure there was ever a plan for the special offering. So I assigned a pair of Vergers to bring the container out and handle moving it around if no one did it. The trouble areas were dealt with and the event went smoothly. All ministries involved responded well to what their duties were that day.

I spent a lot of time discussing Verger assignments. That does not mean everyone else sat around doing nothing. The Acolytes handled their assignments just as every other group that night dealt with their responsibilities. I try to keep duties as simple as possible so there is less nervous energy and more focus on the task at hand. Vergers added a dimension to the service where no one had to overextend themselves for anything. The Vergers dealt with sections of the processions when needed. And in the additional situations where plans were sketchy the ministry of Vergers was flexible to handle that without problems. Vergers do not take away from the ministry of the church. They compliment it.

I shared these two stories for a specific reason. Both showed interaction in a group setting working together. However in one you saw bad collaboration while in the other you saw good collaboration. In the first story you saw a major event being planned. But the person in charge did all the planning himself and did not work with the group to plan out the event better. So when it came to resolving any missing elements that could have been trouble there was a lot of backtracking to handle a situation. In the second story you saw people working together without issues. The plan was in place and resolving potential trouble areas were handled properly without problem.

If you are tasked with being the head of a group running things, recognize first that you cannot do all the work yourself otherwise you will burn yourself out. Heads of major companies do not spend time dealing with sections of departments. They appoint heads to manage those groups of people. And meetings are done with the people designated to run certain areas. Know the plan and be open to solutions to better flesh out the plan for success. The group has to know where they are going to realize your goals.

The two stories involving me mixing in the skills discussed in this chapter. As you know Joseph was used to discuss Interpersonal Skills. Moses took good advice that helped his Organization Skills. Nehemiah showed Planning Skills. Gideon displayed making the most of his resources. If you kept your ego in check and remained humble in helping as well as listening to others Rehoboam is eliminated from the equation. But his story should be a lesson in how not to lead and work with others.

Since I have to deal with two groups of people being able to talk to them the right way is a necessity. Making sure everyone knew what was going on, understanding it, and know what needed to be taken care of was important. The age varied so knowing the right way to talk to someone younger than me, around my age, and older while being respectful had to be established. The main thing in talking to anyone is to be as respectful as possible. You can say something indirectly to insult their intelligence. And if that happens they will tune out anything else you have to say.

When dealing with planning and organizing anything keep the following in mind. No plan is set in stone. Everything is an idea that has to be worked out. See the plan. See where you fit in it. And then see with what is available to you on how to deal with a situation. When you know what is available to you. Then you can figure out where to apply things better. I stated earlier that I used the additional Vergers to compensate for areas we probably were lacking. If you need outside help then use it sparingly. Make the most of what you have first before going there. Your team compliments you. So the group should be organized to fill roles to help you get where you need to go with as little stress as possible.

When tackling big events and situations, ego will probably make you want to do everything yourself. In the short term it may be ok. But in the long run it is not. Identify your skills. What you can do. And what you are lacking. Evaluate the situation and examine who you are as a person. Be honest with yourself and where you stand in a situation. From there you can figure out the best way to handle what is coming your way.

The early church worked together and looked after each other (Acts 4:32-37). In the same way as a group it needs to be established that success depends on how well you come together to achieve goals. My former Martial Arts teacher had a habit of reciting a comment that we would conclude. He would say "We are only as strong—" and we would conclude "—as our weakest link." Recognize the various skills and talent known and not so well known in the group, and find ways of bringing it out to the benefit of others. You will either win as a team or lose as a team. Regardless of how it plays out make sure you put your best effort forward. *"If one member suffers, all suffer together with it; if one member is honored, all rejoice together with it"* (1 Cor. 12:26).

CHAPTER FOUR

Influences and Inspirations

"Whoever walks with the wise becomes wise, but the companion of fools suffers harm" (Prov. 13:20).

You are what you eat: physically, mentally, and spiritually. You need to balance how you fuel yourself. The way you nourish yourself will determine how well you live your life. If you are only feeding yourself garbage you will ultimately become garbage. Physically you need to balance foods the right way. The way you eat and how you approach that is important. Mentally you need to balance entertainment with education. Entertain and educate yourself honestly. Spiritually well that is up to you.

When reading the books of Kings and the events matched in Chronicles in the bible you come across the various rulers of the Kingdom of Israel. The story begins in Kings with the transition from King David to his son King Solomon. During the transition period preparations were being made to build the temple of God. David gave instructions for Solomon in how to follow God. *"And you, my son Solomon, know the God of you father, and serve him with single mind and willing heart; for the LORD searches every mind, and understands every plan and thought. If you seek him, he will be found by you; but if you forsake him, he will abandon you forever"* (1 Chr. 28:9).

Things started out promising in relation to Solomon. But what started out promising took a turn for the worse. Solomon initially started out well. After establishing his rule he followed God. There is even a point early on where he prays to God for wisdom to lead his people. *"Give your servant therefore an understanding mind to govern your people, able to discern between good and evil; for who can govern this your great people"* (1 Kings 3:9).

God would later warn Solomon not to turn away from following him (1 Kings 9:6-7). God also warned Solomon not to intermarry with women of other faiths because they would turn Solomon away from God but Solomon unfortunately didn't listen (1 Kings 11:2). There is a detailed description of what God wanted in rulers listed in Deuteronomy 17:14-20. When Solomon was old his numerous wives turned his heart to their gods and his heart wasn't true to his God. *"So Solomon did what was evil in the sight of the LORD, and did not completely follow the LORD, as his father David had done"* (1 Kings 11:6). In the wake of his death the kingdom was split in two after his son Rehoboam took the throne (1 Kings 12:1-19).

For the duration of the books of Kings the rulers that followed were summed up in two ways. Either they did what was right or what was evil in the sight of the LORD. As people of faith we need to know how to establish a relationship with God. The bible is a telling of history of a people and their relationship (and lack of) with God. We can use this look into the past to help shape our future.

Most biblical figures you read about will have some type of flaw to them. However we can look at both the positives and negatives to help us shape how we should be as individuals. Here are two shining examples that appear in Kings: Hezekiah and Josiah. For the record there were a number of good rulers listed. However when it came to these two the bible points out instances that make them stand out from the others.

First up is King Hezekiah. He appears in 2 Kings 18-20; 2 Chronicles 29-32; and Isaiah 36-39. *"He trusted in the LORD the God of Israel; so that there was no one like him among all the kings of Judah after him, or among those who were before him. For he held fast to the LORD; he did not depart from following him but kept the commandments that the LORD commanded Moses. The LORD was with him; wherever he went, he prospered. He rebelled against the king of Assyria and would not serve him."* (2 Kings 18: 5-7)

All three accounts discuss his reign. Hezekiah was King of Judah. He was known for his religious reforms and surviving the Assyrian invasion. Prior to Hezekiah, King Ahaz set the stage for an Assyrian invasion. While under siege from neighboring countries King Ahaz would look to Assyria for aid (2 Kings 16:5-9). King Ahaz trusted in military alliances and worshipped other gods. When Hezekiah took the throne he ended worship of other gods and returned to the God of his ancestors. He also did not seek political alliances as did Ahaz to boost his strength. He relied on God's protection to get him through things. When the Assyrian army came to invade Judah, Hezekiah turned to Isaiah for advice. And trusting in that advice as well as God, the kingdom survived the invasion.

While leading his reforms he ended idolatry by reopening and cleansing the temple. Worship reached its peak at this time. He even invited the Northern tribes from Israel to come celebrate. As it is recorded in 2 Chronicles 30:26 *"There was great joy in Jerusalem, for since the time of Solomon son of King David of Israel there had been nothing like this in Jerusalem."*

The focus here will be on his walk with God. The bible notes how unique Hezekiah was. Not only does he trust God but he followed the commandments of God completely. In our walk with God how do we approach following his commandments? In order to faithfully follow his commandments we need to study what it is he wants and expects from us. This means taking an honest approach to how we read the bible. The better we read and understand the bible the better we will know how to follow God. The rest is up to you. Church shows you the basics. But the experience is always an individual one.

The second example is King Josiah. Josiah appears in 2 Kings 22:1-23:30; and 2 Chronicles 34-35. *"Before him there was no king like him, who turned to the LORD with all his heart, with all his soul, and with all his might, according to all the law of Moses; nor did any like him arise after him"* (2 Kings 23:25). The bible records that Josiah was also unique among the numerous kings that are recorded in Kings. He lived the Greatest Commandment set by Moses that is recorded in Deuteronomy 6:5 which is *"You shall love the LORD your God with all your heart, and with all your soul, and with all your might."* Josiah did not just follow God. He loved God with all he had just as Moses commanded. So his walk with God was not a mindless zombie doing routines. He did what he did because he truly wanted to. And his behavior was based on the love he had for God.

Josiah was famous in the bible for leading a large campaign of reform back to following God's ideal (2 Kings 23:1-20). This was necessary since after Hezekiah the next two kings (Manasseh and Amon) had undone Hezekiah's accomplishments. Manasseh reversed the reforms performed by Hezekiah. This angered God to the point where he pronounced judgment on the future of Judah (2 Kings 21:10-15).

King Amon continued what Manasseh did and was killed shortly after setting the stage for Josiah. Josiah's efforts halted the skid that was becoming the fall of Judah. Josiah received advice from the prophetess Huldah (1 Kings 22:15-20). She stated that because of the attitude Josiah had towards following God, during his lifetime the kingdom would be spared the calamity that was to come. His campaign was very extensive leading to removing and destroying all pagan worship from the temple and throughout the land. He acted on what was written in the Law of Moses. Like Hezekiah, the bible records that Josiah following his reforms hosted a unique celebration. And it echoed a link to the past. *"No passover like it had been kept in Israel since the days of the prophet Samuel; none of the kings of Israel had kept such a passover as was kept by Josiah, by the priests and the Levites, by all Judah and Israel who were present, and by the inhabitants of Jerusalem"* (2 Chr. 35:18).

Here is an Old Testament figure that gets mentioned in the New Testament named Enoch. Although not much is written about him Enoch stands out as an example of faith and walking with God: *By faith Enoch was taken so that he did not experience death; and "he was not found, because God had taken him." For it was attested before he was taken away that "he had pleased God"* (Heb. 11:5).

Enoch is mentioned among other Old Testament figures in Hebrews chapter 11 when the discussion focuses on faith. Enoch originally appears in Genesis 5:21-23. He lived to be three hundred sixty five years old. Both Genesis and Hebrews state Enoch walked with God. According to Hebrews, Enoch was a man of faith. In order to please God you must have faith. And you must believe God exists. But does simply believing in God enough?

Those familiar with the book of James probably remember the saying 'faith without deeds is dead'. *"For just as the body without the spirit is dead, so faith without works is also dead"* (Jam. 2:26). It is real easy to go through the motions with your responsibilities as Christians. Belief in God is easy. However what type of relationship do you have with God? How are your interactions with people you encounter? How is your lifestyle? This plays a factor in determining your walk with God. In pursuing a relationship with God we need to fall back to David's command to Solomon when he told Solomon to seek God with a willing heart. When you honestly seek a relationship with God you will begin to grow strong in your walk with God. Whatever you lack pray for help it will be provided.

Also as you continue to grow as an individual you need to exercise respect towards each other. There are numerous Christian churches out there with differing fundamentals. However do not let possible clashing beliefs hinder you from growing stronger in your faith and beliefs. Have a foundation for what you believe so you won't fall for or be misled by others. And remember what Jesus said to his disciples when they prevented someone from doing a deed of power in his name. *"Whoever is not against us is for us"* (Mk. 9:40). We may differ from time to time fundamentally but as Christians the core of our beliefs is tied to the teachings of Jesus Christ. We may not always agree with each other but we do need to respect each other.

Speaking of differences, Christianity is not the only belief system devoted to God out there. There are various systems of belief in God out there. *"For all the peoples walk, each in the name of its god, but we will walk in the name of the LORD our God forever and ever"* (Mic. 4:5). Does this mean you trample on others beliefs that are not your own? Of course not, you need to be solid in your beliefs and be mindful and respectful of others differences. One of the Ten Commandments calls on you to love your neighbor as yourself. If that's not enough the Gospels record a conversation where Jesus states the greatest commandment: *"you shall love the Lord your God with all your heart, and with all your soul, and with all your mind, and with all your strength.' The second is this, 'You shall love your neighbor as yourself.' There is no other commandment greater than these"* (Mk. 12:30, 31). Whatever you do in this life if you choose to follow God, have a love for it, and while you are doing that love and respect those around you.

Paul takes this matter a little further in Romans 13:8-10. Paul starts off saying not to owe anyone anything but love. Then explains how loving one another are the fulfillment of the law. For good measure he mentions some of the Ten Commandments and mentions that the commandments that state what not to do can be summed up as loving your neighbor as yourself. *"Love does no wrong to a neighbor; therefore, love is the fulfilling of the law"* (Rom. 13:10).

Some time ago the Vicar Bishop who was leaving my diocese visited my church. In his sermon he shared a story that has stuck with me. He talked about being invited to do a prayer at a gathering that included religious leaders of various faiths. Someone involved with planning the event instructed Bishop not to conclude the prayer with 'in Jesus name'. Apparently the thought was it would offend the other religious leaders gathered that day. The bishop felt it was wrong not to offer prayer in accordance with his faith so he bowed out of praying at the event. It was too late to have his name taken off the list of praying. Someone later substituted for him. Other leaders asked what happened and expected to hear him pray. The bishop explained what happened and why he backed out of praying. The leaders thought it was ridiculous that if the bishop prayed according to his faith it would offend the others gathered.

Another example of shared space was the situation surrounding the Washington National Cathedral following the DC earthquake in 2011. The cathedral like most monuments suffered major damage in the aftermath. Cost of repairs was estimated in the millions. The structure wasn't safe to hold activities in. While the structure was being worked on the cathedral was closed for awhile. In the meantime local places of worship opened their doors offering space for the cathedral to hold services. Not only were they in churches but at times other places of worship.

Also take note that like all lifestyles there are challenges to face. You will face hardships like everyone else. And some of the things you may face could possibly deviate from what you hope to do in your walk with God. *"So I find it to be law that when I want to do what is good; evil lies close at hand"* (Rom. 7:21). In facing any challenges try to reflect on the verses I posted from Titus which appeared in the first chapter titled 'Calling'. When you focus on the positive commands from that verse you can avoid the negatives which will lead to trouble.

Just remember as long as you follow God and remain faithful regardless of the situation, you are never alone. *"do not fear, for I am with you, do not be afraid, for I am your God; I will strengthen you, I will help you, I will uphold you with my victorious right hand"* (Isa. 41:10). When you make the choice to follow God it all starts with faith, then branches out. After establishing faith you must know how to explore it and develop how to share it for the benefit of others. Your actions both great and small demonstrate that. Your walk with God is a journey and during that time you will have moments of growth and understanding.

As you continue on the road as a devout Christian you will learn more where you stand and understand where you need to go. When that happens you can pray more honestly to follow through on the task set before you and be successful. *"I can do all things through him who strengthens me"* (Phil. 4:13).

Just know we do not live like hermits so there are plenty of images and distractions out there that can interfere with our goals. Growing up the conversations always centered on the following: music, sports, videogames, and other forms of entertainment. The more things change the more they stay the same.

Sometimes the only role models and teachers we have is whatever is seen on TV or heard on the radio. That is a double edged sword. That is because it is entertainment and not meant to portray real life. Some programs are used to show aspects of life but are not meant to be imitated or taken literally. But that is what usually happens.

TV has changed over the years. And information is more accessible now than ever before. You were limited on the shows you could watch in the 80's because we only had the network channels. But then cable went to multiple channels which meant more variety in shows and movies you could watch. Most notably being able to watch a movie in its entirety without interruptions or editing for content. That made keeping a show on the air even more of a challenge. Adding to that challenge, you have a show competing with not just sports, but comedy and drama as well. Shows now have to compete with documentaries aired on cable, as well as a large number of reality shows based on all types of situations.

The action and drama shows I grew up with are different from the shows currently on now. If you put a show like "Miami Vice" alongside "24" you notice a big difference in content. There were gunshots and car chases in both shows. However the violence was more detailed in "24". You saw shootings, explosions, and wounds after shootings and stabbings, not to mention scenes of torture. Just as dramas and crime shows have changed over the years so has other areas of entertainment.

Same goes for horror shows. The gore factor is up more even on network shows. However on cable you get away with more skin. Whatever suggestive material was on network channels is more revealing on cable channels. That is not just for action and dramas. That also includes talk and court shows as well. News programming has an effect on you also.

Just make a note that television displays a variety of images. Not all the images shown are good ones. It is a form of entertainment, so do not allow that to be the only influence you have in determining who people are. Or be a factor in determining how you should be as a person. When you develop a foundation of who you are as a person it becomes easier to navigate the numerous images television projects. Balance that foundation and make choices that help you grow and develop as a person on a positive level not leaning on stereotypes.

Pro wrestling has changed over the years. It used to be on Saturday mornings when I was a kid. Given that it was competing against the numerous lineups of Saturday morning cartoons it had to adjust to get attention from those watching Bugs Bunny. These days programming is on during prime time which means now competing with crime dramas, sitcoms, comedies, live sports events, among other types of programming. Adjustments had to be made which at times weren't kid friendly entertainment. The wrestling shows have been able to last because of adjustments to an evening time slot. Some shows jumping to prime time do not last. A popular teen show called "Saved by the Bell" was on during Saturday mornings and enjoyed a decent run for a few years. But when it made a jump to prime time with the "Saved by the Bell: the College Years" that barely lasted a year. The core audience probably tuned in but when it came to attracting a larger audience to make a decent run like its morning program that was not possible.

Pro wrestling shows have some influences in areas of entertainment. For example while watching a Hockey game the night that Stone Cold Steve Austin was a guest host on Monday Night Raw, his theme song was played during a hockey fight. While still in the area of Hockey during the playoff run that saw the Pittsburgh Penguins win the Stanley

Cup. One of the players named Tyler Kennedy when he scored goal at home the fans and the Public Address announcer would chant his name in a similar style to former WWE wrestler Mr. Kennedy. The same way Mr. Kennedy would drag out the 'r' in Mr. and then the 'y' in Kennedy. They did the same for Tyler Kennedy dragging out the 'r' and 'y'. After winning the Super Bowl members of the Green Bay Packers were seen holding WWE championship belts. And some appeared on WWE programming that week. Some people watch pro wrestling and some don't. However it has an influence on people young and old. So those who follow it need to carefully watch the images that are projected there. Wrestling may no longer be kid stuff as it was when on Saturday mornings. But it is still a presence on television. And the images on the shows may not always display something positive. However when you understand what is appropriate and what is not, navigating them becomes easier.

Pro wrestling is sports entertainment so it is labeled as fake. But the hazards these individuals put themselves through is real. It is the same as watching an action sequence in a movie. When characters fight in a movie there is a level of excitement there. When watching violent movies whether it involves gunfights or brawls depending on how it is setup you do get excited.

When action stars like Tony Jaa, Jet Li, Jackie Chan, Donnie Yen, and so on perform fight scenes there is excitement because of their skills as a fighter. When Sylvester Stallone, Arnold Schwarzenegger, Bruce Willis and so on shoot it out with the bad guys there is a level excitement. Even in horror movies you react a certain way to scenes. Violent movies along with dramatic and comedic ones do have an effect and influence on people. However you are still responsible for your own actions. So give allowance to be entertained by the movies, but keep in perspective how you should act and behave.

Videogames have changed over the years. For this book I will view videogames in two eras. The videogames played around the time the original "Tron" movie came out are nowhere near what people have been playing when the sequel "Tron Legacy" came out. The plot from the Tron movies was pretty basic. In the first one the main character gets sucked into the computer world and has to make his way out. In the sequel it is the son of the main character from the first film that gets sucked into the computer world and now has to make his way out. When the original "Tron" came out everyone was likely playing Atari. When "Tron Legacy" came out people were playing Xbox 360, Playstation 3, or Nintendo Wii, or all three systems.

Not only have systems changed over the years but the way we play them has also. When people played an Atari we had a joystick and connected our gaming systems to the antenna on the television set. No one playing that system would expect that years later we would have gaming systems that can play music, movies, let alone connect to the internet for online gaming. The Atari gaming system used a cartridge. And the use of CD's, DVD's, and Blu Ray was not a thought around the time where we played music on cassettes and records, while using videocassettes to play movies. How videogames have been made have gradually changed over the years taking advantage of newer forms of technology. And because of that games are more engaging not to mention addicting. The systems used are more powerful and make the gaming experience more interesting.

When you have games that include voice acting and direction, which is similar to how a cartoon is made that makes a difference. The same goes for the animation of characters both playable and non playable, the technology available now give a more realistic feel. The entertainment value has grown. However because of the degree of how games are produced they can take up a good part of your day and keep you from getting other things taken care of. So balance entertainment with responsibility.

Music also carries influence. Some time ago when my protégé was into music he asked me a number of questions about "old school" hip hop. He based a research paper on our conversation. One question in particular was the difference between how rap is now as opposed to years ago. My first comment was years ago there was more variety. Variety as in everyone did their own thing and there was not a dominant trend. Business didn't have such a strangle hold on the content as it does now.

When you listened to rappers there was a difference in what was being said. You could hear the differences when you heard Kool Moe Dee as opposed to Kool G Rap or even Kool Keith. Masta Ace did not sound like Master P. The Fresh Prince did not sound like Doug E. Fresh. Ice T did not sound like Ice Cube. Redhead Kingpin did not sound like Redman. Smooth B did not sound like CL Smooth. Craig G did not sound like Craig Mack. Big Daddy Kane did not sound like Big L or Big Punisher. Lords of the Underground did not sound like Digital Underground. Naturally I'm playing with names here but the point is there is a difference in styles when you listened to rappers. People were not just repeating what others were doing at the time. There was more originality to what was being done. Even with the female rappers you could tell the difference from Queen Latifah, MC Lyte, Salt n Pepa, and so on.

Recently Ice T did a documentary called "Something from Nothing: Art of Rap". Over the course of the film he had various conversations with other rappers about how they do what they do. In discussing variety I will focus on the comments from Doug E. Fresh. In that conversation Doug E talked about three individuals who he considers to be the greatest MC's. They were Kool Moe Dee, Grandmaster Caz, and Melle Mel. When he describes Kool Moe Dee style he mentions that it was technically extreme and sharp. When he describes Grandmaster Caz style he mentions it being slickness and flavor. And when it comes to Melle Mel it's spiritual. And in each case he recites verses to prove that fact.

Speaking of Melle Mel during his acceptance speech at the Rock and Roll Hall of Fame he made a memorable comment. He asked the recording industry to do more to restore Hip Hop to the culture of music and art that it once was. And move away from the culture of violence that it has become. He went on to mention that he was never shot or arrested for what he does.

It is easy to go back 5, 10, or even 20 years to find some act of violence related to Hip Hop. In the documentary "Rap Sheet: Hip Hop and the Cops" they examined the fact that the police department has a book called a dossier that lists rappers and a lot of personal information about them. A dossier is a collection of documents of information about a person or incident. Rapper Lil' Cease appears in the documentary. During his interview he mentions how following the shooting of Notorious B.I.G. they were shown pictures at the police station of them at the event before the shooting. This was echoed from a previous documentary he appeared in titled "Biggie and Tupac" where he mentions seeing photos from that night. Essentially it showed that police have rappers under surveillance. The origin of the famous dossier is explored in "Black and Blue: Legends of the Hip Hop Cop". The police officer responsible for collecting the information that ended up in the book was interviewed.

Rappers are storytellers. Telling stories is not a problem. Selling stories as truth of your lifestyle, while talking about drugs and violence is a problem. It's safe to say rappers talking about violence and drug use are probably not doing it at the drop of a hat. However given the connection Rap has with violence and drug use it is easy to be suspect of any altercation that comes up. So anyone talking freely about that type of content might as well stand in front the police station with a big sign that says "ARREST ME!" No harm may be intended but just know whatever image you display there will be someone who will check to see if you are who you claim to be or faking it. Like a typical Western you will be called out to see if what you are doing is real.

Forms of entertainment should not be responsible for people's actions as a whole. But entertainers of any kind should carry themselves with some level of responsibility. When people are following you the power you have needs to be used with caution. They may not expect to be setting an example but chances are they will be one way or another.

In the end it is not them who are responsible for what you do. It is all on you. The choices you make will determine the outcome more that any form of influence whether it be entertainment or otherwise.

In Ezekiel chapter 18 the bulk of it lays out that we are accountable for our own actions. As the chapter unfolds God declares that both parent and child are his but the person who sins will die. Good or bad it is our choices and ours alone. You are not responsible for anyone else's actions but yours. Your parents are only accountable for their actions. Whatever they did is on them. And whatever you do is only on you. *"The person who sins shall die. A child shall not suffer for the iniquity of a parent, nor a parent suffer for the iniquity of a child; the righteousness of the righteous shall be his own, and the wickedness of the wicked shall be his own"* (Ezek. 18:20).

The chapter is laid out as follows. In Ezekiel 18:5-9 it states that a person who does right will live. Then in Ezekiel 18:10-13 it states that if the person has a child who does wrong the child will die. In Ezekiel 18:14-18 it states that if the child sees the parent doing wrong but avoids that path the child will live. But the parent will die. In Ezekiel 18:21-23 it states that if the wicked turn from their evil ways and do right, they will not die. All will be forgiven and forgotten by God. In Ezekiel 18:24 it states that if the righteous turn and do wrong, whatever good they did will be forgotten. And they will be punished for the wrong they did.

Not everyone has a squeaky clean personal history. Then again no one is truly innocent. If you have personal demons you had to battle years ago so be it. The question should not be what you have done. But why you did it, and how you changed. If you changed for the better then past history should just be that. THE PAST! Every experience good and bad made you who you are. And you should use that to empower you to act better and to do right by others. Not cower and say you are worthless. If you have truly committed to changing your ways then stick to it. Let go of what happened and move on.

Don't ever feel that you are beyond redemption. If you are familiar with the crucifixion of Jesus then you remember there were two criminals hanging on the cross along with him. In Luke's account of the crucifixion (Lk. 23:39-43) there is more of an exchange between the criminals and Jesus. And those who follow the Holy Week traditions likely have been in church on Good Friday where they reflect on the words said on the cross. One of the criminals derides him asking for Jesus to save them. While the other states that they deserve the punishment they are getting and that Jesus is innocent of what is being done to him. After one of the criminals speaks kindly to Jesus, the response from Jesus is: *"Truly I tell you, today you will be with me in Paradise"* (Lk. 23:43). That criminal showed an act of repentance.

Paul states in Romans that the wages of sin is death (Rom. 6:23). However repentance is turning away from whatever sin you have committed. Good examples of repentance can be found with King David (2 Sam. 12:13, and 2 Sam. 24:10). When David is confronted with the wrong he did instead of ignoring it he recognized and admitted what he did wrong then took steps to correct it. *"For godly grief produces a repentance that leads to salvation and brings no regret, but worldly grief produces death"* (2 Cor. 7:10).

Another example of people who made a change for the better is the Apostle Paul. We first meet him as Saul of Tarsus. When he first appears in the book of Acts he seems destined to become one of the villains in the bible. Saul is at first persecuting the church (Acts 8:1-3). Saul later to become Paul reflects on how he persecuted the church in some of his letters (1 Cor. 15:9; Gal. 1:13; Phil. 3:6; and 1 Tim. 1:13).

But on the trip to Damascus his life changed. He went from persecuting the church to being one of the leaders. His conversion almost didn't happen. During the journey to Damascus Saul was struck blind and entered into a conversation with Jesus (Acts 9:3-6). The people with him were not sure what was going on but ended up leading Saul to the city. Ananias was called by Jesus to lay hands on Saul to restore his sight (Acts 9:10-12).

However Ananias was reluctant to do so knowing the bad reputation Saul had. *"Lord, I have heard from many about this man, how much evil he had done to your saints in Jerusalem; and here he has authority from the chief priests to bind all who invoke your name"* (Acts 9:13, 14). But Jesus responded saying that Saul had a specific call and was needed. And will be instructed in what he needed to do in his ministry. After that Ananias then did what was required of him and helped Saul recover his sight (Acts 9:17-19).

In the book of Revelation there are a lot of images that appear some clear and some confusing. In that book however repent appears in at least seven verses (Rev. 2:5; 2:16; 3:3; 9:20; 9:21; 16:9; 16:11). The first three verses repent appears in is a call for change. So the verse would read like a progress report that goes: you are doing well however you are lacking in certain areas, change the following things or you will be in trouble. The last four verses that repent appears in, the writer is making note of a failure to change. At this point in Revelation the writer is making note that despite being punished people didn't repent. Which means at least two things first is that it's never too late to change, and second people need to have the desire to change. *"The Lord is not slow about his promise, as some think of slowness, but is patient with you, not wanting any to perish, but all to come to repentance"* (2 Pet. 3:9).

There is a movie starring Ving Rhames called "Saving God". In it he plays a man on parole who became a minister while in prison. Upon getting out he sets off to restore a church in a drug infested neighborhood. Over the course of the movie you found out how he ended up in prison. And while trying to help a young drug dealer change his ways he shares that story with him. The young man he is trying to help ends up attempting to change leaving his life of crime behind. But his boss named Blaze won't let him and things take a turn for the worst.

At the end of the movie there is the confrontation between the minister and the Blaze. Blaze walks into church holding a gun and it appears he wants to kill the minister. The two start talking. And eventually Blaze draws his gun as if to shoot. However Blaze admits he wants to abandon his life of crime. Laying down his gun he asks if the minister can help him change. The minister says gladly. In the end they kneel down to pray. *"You were taught to put away your former way of life, your old self, corrupt and deluded by its lusts, and to be renewed in the spirit of your minds, and to clothe yourselves with the new self, created according to the likeness of God in true righteousness and holiness"* (Eph. 4:22-24).

Statistics, news, religion, stereotypes, etc. all say something. However do not let your life be ruled by them. As much stuff as they say or imply it is still up to you how you live your life. The choices and decisions you make play a part and lead to what is going on now with you. Win or lose, your life is YOUR life so live it responsibly and with no regrets.

We have talked to a degree about choosing to follow a path with God, various forms of entertainment, and to an extent responsibility. Now the focus will be on how to treat people. At my regular job I was once asked about the importance of there being a holiday for Martin Luther King. In the beginning it was hard to explain. To borrow part of a line from a speech from the former NAACP president Myrlie Evers-Williams at the National Convention for the National Society of Black Engineers at Kansas City in 1999. When it came to the attacks on Affirmative Action she said "it didn't just benefit black people". The same can be said about Martin Luther King. He was not just a benefit to black people. He did not just march for better rights when it came to race. He was also out there supporting union workers as well as others in his fight for equal treatment. My wish every year around the time of his birthday is that the focus is not just on singing "We shall overcome", and reciting the "I have a dream" speech. Thankfully there are events on that day which helps explain it. There are two days in January for his birthday. One is his actual birthday the other is the observed holiday. To understand why there is a holiday you need to first understand how it became established as a holiday.

A few years ago the rap group Public Enemy did a video to a song in reaction as to how some states at the time wasn't recognizing the birthday as a national holiday. The song was called "By the time I get to

Arizona". My former Rector used to walk around clutching a worn copy of the book about King called "Testament of Hope". He looked up to King and always took a moment to acknowledge the accomplishments made by the late civil rights leader. He made some inspiring sermons those weekends.

I was in elementary school when his birthday became a national holiday. Memories that come to mind are the book reports I had to do talking about segregation, sit in, boycotts, all the while not having a clue what any of that was about. Let alone able to spell and pronounce some of those words. Growing up I never experienced racism on that level. There were no 'white only' bathrooms or white sections of towns when I was growing up. I did not have to deal with sitting only in the back of the bus or movie theatres. My home was never fire bombed. Burning crosses were not planted in front my home. And there definitely are no stories about lynching. My parents, grandparents, and great grandparents probably have stories about these experiences. In understanding what they went through it makes me more grateful for what I have now. My great-great grandparents were the transition out of slavery generation.

King had an approach of nonviolence to help bring about change. He staged peaceful protests to bring about change to unjust laws. This was met with unpleasant opposition and numerous arrests. He lived under constant danger. His home was attacked. He received numerous death threats, almost fatally stabbed, and was jailed several times. He truly lived what was said by Paul in Romans 12:18 *"If it is possible, so far as it depends on you, live peaceably with all."*

Protesters today only have to deal with a fraction of what people during the Civil Rights movement went through. Images from the Civil Rights movement that stuck with me from elementary school days were those of people being sprayed with firehouses and attacked by police dogs. When glancing at his life it almost resembles the life of the early apostles. The Apostle Paul comes to mind at the moment. Paul discusses his struggles in 2 Corinthians 11:23-30. During his struggles he mentions numerous imprisonments, floggings, near death experiences, beatings, stoning, shipwreck, dangers from bandits and other people, among other hardships.

It may seem that having a nonviolent approach is ineffective. And if you read through history there are a number of violent clashes and wars that occurred. There are a number of wars listed in the bible as well. However there is a dispute that was resolved in a peaceful manner. Elisha helped end a war that was going on between Aram and Israel in 2 Kings 6:8-23. Elisha was giving the King of Israel advice on how to thwart plans by the King of Aram. The King of Aram would later come up with a plan to deal with Elisha. As the plan unfolded Elisha with God's assistance struck the soldiers blind and led them into the hands of the King of Israel. Despite having the soldiers of Aram at his mercy, Elisha suggested that the soldiers be treated kindly and sent home. The story concludes as follows: *"...And the Arameans no longer came raiding into the land of Israel"* (2 Kings 6:23). Violence leads to more violence until someone either gives up or dies. Here instead of a violent confrontation that would have probably escalated into a larger problem. An act of kindness presented the right way led to a peaceful resolution.

When Barack Obama was running for president in 2008 there was a number of references to King. There have also been numerous images of those two together. When Obama won the election it was a moment for those of my parents generation and earlier who went through the experiences during and after the Civil Rights movement that felt an event like that will never happen. Others have run before in the President elections. I was a kid when Jesse Jackson ran for President. However Barack Obama was the first one to win. How he will be viewed in the years to come is open to debate.

Two years later in 2010 when the Washington National Cathedral hosted their annual National Acolyte Festival in Washington DC. That year was unique because it was also the host of the annual National Conference for the Vergers Guild of the Episcopal Church. That week during a series of workshops, meetings, and tours, participants at the conference got a good look at the cathedral. That weekend was the

National Acolyte Festival so the Acolytes from my church were reunited with me that day. Following the events of the festival I pointed to two areas in the cathedral. First was the pulpit that is said to be the site where Dr. Martin Luther King Jr. preached his last sermon prior to being shot. The second area was where President Barack Obama knelt to pray during his Inauguration. Interestingly enough after making a comment about the pulpit in October of 2010 two months later it was announced that our church would host the annual service commemorating the life of Dr. Martin Luther King Jr. In the service bulletin at the end there is a comment mentioning that he preached in Washington National Cathedral prior to his death later on that week.

A lot has changed since the days of King. We have benefited from the events of the Civil Rights movement. Following the service held at my church, I went out to lunch with a fellow Verger who aided me at the event. When we sat down to eat I made a comment that a hundred years ago this wouldn't be happening. And she realized what I meant. A hundred years ago if a black man so much as looked at a white woman he would likely be found hanging from a tree somewhere.

Casually walking into a public restaurant to eat was unheard of back then. If segregation still existed the way it did years ago, when it came to going to conferences with fellow Vergers in the south. Chances are I would end up eating my food outdoors while my white counterparts enjoyed sitting down to a table to eat. Thankfully segregation along those lines no longer exists and the ability to fellowship with other vergers despite race is fairly open. And the solidarity and support for one another is not hindered because of biased laws.

King had his share of critics as well. The late Dr. John Henrik Clarke talks about King in his documentary "A Great and Mighty Walk." Dr. Clarke praises King as a theologian. But points out he agreed with the use of nonviolence as a strategy, not a way of life. King is not the only example of being a hero or role model. There are a number of heroes past and present that can be used. When choosing a hero to emulate make sure that person is of good moral character. Note I said choose a hero to emulate with a good moral character. This doesn't mean you alienate friends and family. When you understand the path you are going on and are determined to go there, the only person that can stop you is you.

On the heels of the recent services commemorating the life of Martin Luther King Jr. as well as the service for Absalom Jones a former slave turned minister, there were numerous references to the movie "Twelve Years a Slave". It is based on the book that is a memoir of Solomon Northrup. As is known Solomon was kidnapped and sold into slavery. The memoir is an account of Solomon's experience as a slave and eventually being rescued from his situation. You get to see the highs and lows of that experience. He gives a fair account and states it is not an antislavery book.

The movie adaption was not going to capture everything that happened in the book. There was research done and naturally some liberties taken with how the book became a film. Some events were cut out and some events that are not in the book were added in. For example there is a scene in the movie showing Solomon strolling down the street with his family heading to the store to buy something. And a man that we later find out is a slave that is not able to freely travel into a store. That showed the contrast of how a free man lives as opposed to a slave. The subject matter whether reading the book or watching the movie will not paint a pleasant picture since it shows at times man's inhumanity towards each other.

Getting back to the recent church services, the main comments during the sermons were how far we came since the days of slavery. This echoed a dilemma I faced while in college a few years ago. While in college one of the toughest tests for me as a Christian was how to reconcile my beliefs as a black person given the role of Christianity in Slavery. As well as the fact that Slavery is in the bible. The entire time I have been in the church there has never been a discussion about slavery mentioned in the bible or how to deal with that. Involvement in black student groups posed a challenge because they showed many reasons to denounce my ties to the Christian faith.

Following the service for Absalom Jones I revisited what I remembered reading in the book "Twelve Years a Slave". Solomon was sold into slavery and his name was changed to Platt. Despite the obstacles he prospered due to his various skills. After awhile Solomon saw freedom and was reunited with his family. The story shares parallels with a biblical account of another person. Solomon Northrup's story mirrors the account of Old Testament figure Joseph. Joseph was sold into Slavery by his brothers (Gen. 37:27, 28). Joseph was enslaved and later imprisoned for 15 years. His name was changed when he entered into service of the Pharaoh (Gen. 41:45). Despite the circumstances Joseph prospered in life and eventually saw his family again. What strikes me about the story of Joseph was that while in the service of Pharaoh the people become slaves to him. But the way it happens made me take a different view of the bible's approach to slavery.

Joseph was in service to the Pharaoh aiding to avoid problems due to famine. So in Genesis chapter 47 you see how Joseph managed the affairs of the people dealing with the situation. There are three exchanges that come up. When the famine comes people exchanged money for food (Gen. 47:13, 14). When they had no money they exchanged livestock for food (Gen. 47:16, 17). When they had no livestock they offered themselves as slaves in exchange for food (Gen. 47: 19). In the exchanges you notice that people offered something for food. By the time you see slavery mentioned for food it was in an effort to avoid starving. When that debt was paid they were free to go.

This made me take another look at slavery in the bible. Before continuing I want it known that this is not an effort to show I support or condone the usage of slavery in any form inside or out of the bible. Slavery existed in the time of the Old Testament. And it was around during the times of the New Testament. Slavery in ancient times existed mostly in these forms: debt slavery, punishment for a crime, and enslavement of prisoners of war.

Slavery took on various forms over the centuries. Some parts remained the same while others were different. Because the topic of slavery leaves a bad taste in most people's mouths it is hard to really hold a conversation that is not antagonistic. However if we are to reconcile any relation to slavery an honest conversation must be had one way or another.

"Whoever kidnaps a person, whether that person has been sold or is still held in possession, shall be put to death" (Ex. 21:16). Slaves brought to America were brought against their will to work. In Ancient Israel if you could not provide for yourself or your family you sold yourself into slavery so you would not starve. There are rules about slavery in the bible (Ex. 21:1-11) but it was to protect the slave. Because of the numerous images in the bible it is easy to manipulate and distort things to suit anyone's purpose. Solomon Northrup mentions Peter Tanner who does not appear in the movie using Luke 12:47 to justify how bad he can beat slaves. A simplified version of the conversation was said by Edwin Epps the master whom Solomon spent the remaining ten years of his time as a slave under in the movie "Twelve Years a Slave".

When you get to the New Testament there are verses in the letters of Paul calling on slaves to obey their masters (Eph. 6:5-8, and Col. 3:22-25). However next to that are verses calling on masters to treat their slaves fairly (Eph. 6:9, and Col. 4:1). Another point of contention is the letter Philemon. It is a letter Paul wrote to a slave master on behalf of a runaway slave.

The runaway slave happens to be named Onesimus. Onesimus appears in Colossians 4:9 *"he is coming with Onesimus, the faithful and beloved brother, who is one of you. They will tell you about everything here."* Onesimus is named as one of the members coming to lend a hand. The letter Philemon is used by both people for and against slavery. When you read the letter from start to finish you will notice that Paul is at first discussing Philemon's ties to the Christian faith (Philem. 1:4-7). Then he offers an appeal to Philemon on behalf of Onesimus *"I am appealing to you for my child, Onesimus, whose father I have become during my imprisonment"* (Philem. 1:10). Paul notes that he found Onesimus useful in his ministry but out of respect to Philemon is sending Onesimus back and won't do anything further without consent. (Philem. 1:12-14). Similar to someone having a parent fill out a consent form on behalf of a child. He concludes his appeal for kindness to Onesimus by asking Philemon to accept Onesimus back not just as a slave but as a fellow brother. Paul concludes his plea by asking that Onesimus be forgiven for any wrong doing (Philem. 1:16-18). Paul may be sending a slave back to his owner. But he is at the same time appealing to the master to look kindly on his slave and treat him fairly despite being a runaway. Runaway slaves were treated harshly even in those times. We don't know from the letter what had happened to Onesimus. But we can fully tell that Paul defends his friend and hopes things will turn out ok for him.

The bible mentions slavery a number of times. But the use of slavery had a different tone than that on Africans brought to America. Unfortunately because of the treatment of slaves in America we know the crueler, racist usage. Getting back to "Twelve Years a Slave" both the book and the movie. The book is a detailed account of one man's journey through slavery. The movie focused on certain parts in the book. The research done and added made a better picture of what regularly went on at that time. There were good and bad points to be seen. In the book Solomon Northrup points out varying viewpoints of how people viewed Slavery whether they are from the north or south. He also mentions slave masters both good and bad. While reading the book you find not all masters were cruel. And because of the various skills he had at times he was loaned out to others to help aid in working.

Given that slaves in America could not read or write they were dependant on others who could read. It is unfortunate about how religion was involved in slavery. We cannot change what others did centuries ago. We can change what we do from here on out. Some may argue that religion was forced on people as a means of control. However there is a redeeming fact that religion used the right way can empower a person giving them strength. There are numerous images projected at you in a given time. Take a moment to sort out fact from fiction and then make your own choice in what you will do. *"Now if you are unwilling to serve the LORD, choose this day whom you will serve, whether the gods your ancestors served in the region beyond the River or the gods of the Amorites in whose land you are living; but as for me and my household, we will serve the LORD"* (Josh. 24:15).

History is a combination of the good, the bad, and the ugly. You are not going to like what you see all the time. However avoid doing finger pointing about someone's faults. Learn from their mistakes so you do not repeat them in the future. Times have changed. However racism still exists in the world. Fortunately it is not as blunt as years ago. We have a responsibility to understand where we came from and how to resolve our differences in a peaceful manner. The race issues will still come up. There is a lot we can learn from the past so that we can avoid making the same mistakes in the present and future. The good and bad examples have a lot to teach us. Learn what the good parts did right and focus on their examples moving forward. Look at the bad areas and learn from their mistakes so you avoid repeating them in the future. *"One who forgives an affront fosters friendship, but the one who dwells on disputes will alienate a friend"* (Prov. 17:9).

In recent times the shooting deaths of unarmed young black men have made headlines. Whether it was Trayvon Martin or Jordan Davis being shot to death, both events has led to shock and outrage. One of the unfortunate things I learned growing up is that there is a mentality that young men in my race are all criminals. Whenever I walk into a store all eyes are on me expecting to steal something. Most times when I walk in and attract unnecessary attention I walk out. One time after church dressed in slacks, shirt and tie I walked into a store to buy a notepad. The security guard decided to follow me around the store and circled the aisle I was in.

Ironically he was at first by the television screens and could have just watched me on the monitors. But he decided to go the extra mile and follow me. Instead of walking out I continued to do what I planned on doing. After buying a notepad I walked past the guard and gave him a business card inviting him to come visit my church. Since he made the effort to follow me around the store he probably would not have a problem coming to my church. He had no idea that he was following around a church official. He just saw a young man and assumed despite being dressed nice that I was a criminal. That mentality about young men in my race will not go away anytime soon. But steps can be taken to weather that and still do what you need to do. Interestingly that was the last time I saw him at that store. Racism and prejudice are not easy topics to discuss or deal with. However we can make an effort to understand one another so issues can be resolved with few problems.

When you set on the path you choose as an individual make sure the foundation you establish is solid. When it comes to your beliefs, and ideals a solid foundation will establish solid roots for you as a person to fall back on. Luke discusses two foundations (Lk. 6:46-49). Jesus mentions there are two ways of responding to his words. The one who hears his words and acts on it is like a person who builds a house on a solid foundation. Because of the solid foundation the house was not moved by flooding of the river. *"That one is like a man building a house, who dug deeply and laid the foundation on rock; when a flood arose, the river burst against that house but could not shake it, because it had been well built"* (Lk. 6:48). A person who hears his words and does not act is like someone who builds a house on a poor foundation and when the river flooded destroyed the house. You do not want anything destroyed so you should take careful steps to build it right. When establishing your faith and beliefs take a care to build it on solid ground.

Being by the book is ok from the standpoint that you have standards and likely a solid foundation. However that should not stop you from being flexible and tolerant of others differences. We cannot choose our families or those we encounter. But we can learn to understand each other's differences and viewpoints in an effort to better work with each other. Compromise is not weakness it is cooperation hoping to achieve better success. You can still maintain your values while dealing with others who are willing to deal with you.

Whatever trials and challenges lay ahead for you, hopefully you will succeed. *"Blessed are you when people revile you and persecute you and utter all kinds of evil against you falsely on my account"* (Matt. 5:11). Think about stories from the bible when the Israelites were in captivity. There are three stories in the book of Daniel that come to mind.

The first story to be focused on is the arrival in the Babylonian Court. The focus will be around Daniel 1:3-20. Daniel along with others was brought in to be educated for a period of time. *"The king assigned them a daily portion of the royal rations of food and wine. They were to be educated for three years, so that at the end of that time they could be stationed in the king's court"* (Dan. 1:5). What type of food were the royal rations? It is not clear from the text. Whatever type of food it was Daniel did not agree with it. So a compromise was attempted. Daniel would ask the palace master to allow them to have something else to eat in place of the rations instead. *"But Daniel resolved that he would not defile himself with the royal rations of food and wine; so he asked the place master to allow him not to defile himself"* (Dan. 1:8).

This however was met with a challenge since the palace master feared for his life thinking Daniel and the others would be worst off. Daniel offered a test that they should be allowed to eat that way, and if things turned out bad a change back to the daily rations would be allowed (Dan. 1:12-17). After the testing with vegetables and water, Daniel and the others appeared healthier and better off than the others. So the palace master continued to allow them to eat what they have been eating. Choosing to have healthy eating habits comes with a set of challenges. However if it proves to benefit you in the long run people might get behind it. Remember to take care of yourself health wise.

The second story involves the fiery furnace. The focus will be on Daniel chapter 3. The king made a Golden Image and gave order that whoever did not worship the image will be thrown into the furnace. All paid homage with a few exceptions. People noted that certain people refused to follow that order and was brought to the king's attention: *"There are certain Jews whom you have appointed over the affairs of the province of Babylon: Shadrach, Meshach, and Abednego. These pay no heed to you, O king. They do not serve your gods and they do not worship the golden statue that you have set up"* (Dan. 3:12).

When brought before the king to answer for their actions. The king ordered them to pay homage to the image he set up or be thrown into the furnace. Even when their lives were threatened by the king the individuals refused to bow to the image. They would declare that even if it meant death they would not bow down to the golden image. *"If our God whom we serve is able to deliver us from the furnace of blazing fire and out of your hand, O king, let him deliver us. But if not, be it known to you, O king, that we will not serve your gods and we will not worship the golden statue that you have set up"* (Dan. 3:17, 18).

The men were bound and put into the furnace. However despite the men being thrown in the furnace the king noticed that the men seemed unharmed and that someone appeared to be in there with them. When he called for them to come out, it was noted that the men were unharmed by the flames. Following that the king had respect for them and their God. *"Therefore I make this decree: Any people, nation, or language that utters blasphemy against the God of Shadrach, Meshach, and Abednego shall be torn limb from limb, and their houses laid in ruins; for there is no other god who is able to deliver in this way"* (Dan. 3:29). Choosing to follow your beliefs will have its fair share of challenges. People will challenge you from within and outside your beliefs. That may force you into uncomfortable situations. However stay true to what you believe regardless of what others say and keep at it. As long as you continue to grow as an individual in your beliefs you will be able to prosper despite whatever is going on.

The third story involves the Daniel in the Lion's Den. The focus will be on Daniel 6:3-24. It deals with integrity to an extent. At this point Daniel was well established in his area. The king planned on appointing Daniel above all in the kingdom. The other established leaders tried to bring up charges against Daniel but found there was no type of corruption to use on him. Legally they could not find anything false about Daniel so they tried to find something to use against him in regards to his faith. *"...We shall not find any ground for complaint against this Daniel unless we find it in connection with the law of his God"* (Dan. 6:5).

The leaders came up with the idea to have the king sign into law that if anyone is caught praying to anything aside from the king for thirty days, that person is to be thrown to the lions. Despite knowing this law was passed Daniel continued his habits of praying to God. The conspirators caught Daniel doing this and told the king. When the king heard the news he was distressed and tried all he could to save Daniel from punishment. However the conspirators kept reminding him of the law that was passed. The king finally gave the command to have Daniel sent to the lion's den.

The next morning the king rushed to the lion's den and called out to Daniel hoping nothing happened to him. Daniel answered back *"My God sent his angel and shut the lions' mouths so that they would not hurt me, because I was found blameless before him; and also before you, O king, I have done no wrong"* (Dan. 6:22). At that point the king was delighted to know Daniel was safe. And after having Daniel released he ordered the conspirators into the lion's den along with their families.

As long as you have the truth on your side there is nothing to fear. *"Whoever speaks the truth gives honest evidence, but a false witness speaks deceitfully"* (Prov. 12:17). Live an honest life and you will not have to worry about any wrongdoing directed at you. The truth will come out one way or another. And once it is out anyone guilty of wrong doing will be in trouble.

Your actions speak louder than words. Jesus echoed these sentiments when the disciples of John the Baptist asked if he was the one (Lk. 7:18-23). When the disciples asked if Jesus was the one or should they expect another. Jesus gave examples of what he has done instead of stating yes or no. *"Go and tell John what you have seen and heard: the blind receive their sight, the lame walk, the lepers are cleansed, the deaf hear the dead are raised, the poor have good news brought to them"* (Lk. 7:22). Early on in this chapter while discussing faith there was the famous verse from James 1:26 about faith without works are dead. It also says in James 2:18 *"I by my works will show you my faith."* Your thoughts and actions say a lot about you directly and indirectly. The image you display is not just in the clothes you wear or the items you possess. It is in the way you carry yourself and how you treat others. How you treat others verbally and physically tells people more about the type of person you are without you saying a word about yourself.

This chapter spoke at length about choosing to follow God and finding your true self. That journey is an individual one. Many images will be thrown at you some good and some bad. It is not easy to sort out what is right for you because what people may think is right for you might not be what you need at that time. In order to follow God you need to figure out what that means for you in how you approach that. When it comes to race you cannot just simply go along with someone that looks like you. Make sure they reflect what is healthy and right for you. A form of entertainment is just that entertainment. Do not let what entertainers are doing be the only influence in your life. They are human just like you with just as many flaws. That also goes for public leaders. The examples given of some leaders in the bible showed the positives and negatives in their lives. Learn what they did right and wrong. Then make it a point to focus on the right things so you can prosper.

It takes work to establish your identity as an individual let alone as a Christian. *"The one who thus serves Christ is acceptable to God and has human approval. Let us then pursue what makes for peace and for mutual upbuilding"* (Rom. 14:18, 19). Holding true to yourself and maintaining your faith regardless of what is thrown at you is another challenge altogether. Whether or not you established your identity there will always be challenges great and small. In this chapter you were given an idea of how to approach having a relationship with God. There were a number of examples of individuals in the bible who had good relationships with God that you can study and learn from.

Life will have its fair set of challenges both major and minor. Some will be easily dealt with. Some will take time to deal with. And some will be occasional situations. As long as you continue to grow as an individual honestly understanding who you are as a person. Whatever situations may come up you should be able to deal with. *"Indeed, all who want to live a godly life in Christ Jesus will be persecuted"* (2 Tim. 3:12).

CHAPTER FIVE

"The human spirit will endure sickness; but a broken spirit—who can bear" (Prov. 18:14).

There are times when things will not go right. And it will likely test your patience, faith, let alone beliefs. All you can do is try and stay true to who you are and hope that things will get better. The previous chapters were about developing who you are as a person, individual growth, team building, and to a degree leadership development. This chapter is all about handling stressful situations. At these times it is real easy to become a one man show and rely on your own strength. But you must put your ego aside and tap into your resources for help. Some things you can handle yourself. And some you cannot. Just do not try and carry all of it on your own. Hopefully this chapter helps you find peace in whatever strife you may be going through currently or sometime later.

The best know example of suffering comes from the book of Job. Job losses everything you possibly could lose. He lost his wealth, family, and even health. When Job suffers losses his wife asks why doesn't he curse and die. Job's response was should he only accept the good and not the bad. At times during our life we may sound like Job. *"If only my anguish could be weighed and all my misery be placed on the scales"* (Job 6:2 NIV). We may feel that life sucks, or that there is no help, moments of restlessness, as well as moments of anguish. Despite whatever grief or despair you may be going through don't give in.

There are lessons we can take from Job. Despite the writing of the book of Job being centuries older than any of us, the themes are still visible today. At some point someone might have had wished they were dead. *"Why did I not perish at birth, and die as I came from the womb"* (Job 3:11 NIV). Or feel there was no help at all. *"In truth I have no help in me, and any resource is driven from me"* (Job 6:13). Or maybe there have been some moments of restlessness. *"When I lie down I say, 'When shall I rise?' But the night is long, and I am full of tossing until dawn"* (Job 7:4). Possibly there have been some moments of anguish and frustration. *"Yet if I speak, my pain is not relieved; and if I refrain, it does not go away"* (Job 16:6 NIV). Maybe God is angry with you. *"He has torn me in his wrath, and hated me; he has gnashed his teeth at me; my adversary sharpens his eyes against me"* (Job 16:9).

While asking the question 'Why me'. You can gain comfort from reading and studying the book of Job. While reading you find there is no compact explanation as to why people suffer. The book gives insights into reasons for suffering. Here are some other things biblically you can learn from dealing with suffering.

For starters some suffering is caused by Satan. In the first two chapters of Job you notice God did not cause Job's problems. He allowed them, Satan caused the pain. Another point is suffering is not always the result of sin. It can be pointed out that if you do wrong expect to be punished. And Job's friends clearly expressed that viewpoint in the conversations. But sin is not always the reason for bad things happening. In John 9:1-5 Jesus heals a man born blind. When the disciples ask Jesus who sinned causing the man to be born blind, his answer was none.

Another point is good intentions could cause more problems. Job's friends at first did the right thing coming to look in on their friend.

They found their friend in silent grief and sat collectively in silent grief with him. Unfortunately their attitude and sense of being right prevented them from being useful to their friend's situation. They had their own ideas and solutions as to why Job was suffering. Instead of listening to their friend discuss what was bothering him. They instead focused on their theories and tried to prove they were right. In the end arguments erupted and the friends were at odds with each other for a lengthy period of time.

If you are trying to be there for your friend, be there. Listen to them when they speak, then react. Do not come in as a know it all. Find out where they are coming from so that you can give the right response. And sometimes the best response is none. Let a hurting person speak their mind and get out their anguish. His friends frustrated Job to the point where he told them to be quiet. *"If you would only keep silent, that would be your wisdom"* (Job 13:5).

That was a general view on suffering. In the end no one has all the answers on suffering. It happens and all you can do is deal with it as best as you can. Your character will be defined on how well you manage the situation. There are various forms of suffering that an individual goes through. The main ones that will be discussed here are: grief, depression, suicide, betrayal, and bullying. Despite the heaviness of topics like grief, depression, and suicide, there will be an effort made to keep the topics light and not be a downer.

Loss is a painful experience to anyone. *"Blessed are those who mourn, for they will be comforted"* (Matt. 5:4). All kinds of emotions will come into play here. And at times it may feel like it will never let up. Trust that these feelings you are having are a normal reaction to loss. There is no right or wrong way to grieve, however there are ways to help cope with the pain you are experiencing so that in time you can gradually move on.

Grieving is a personal and individual experience. How you react to it depends on factors such as your personality, experiences in this matter, the nature of the loss, and your faith. The process of grief takes time and you must be patient and let the healing process run its course. There is no set time for when you truly will be over the mourning process of a loved one. It may be days, months, or over a year. Just try to remain calm during this time and let the recovery period naturally happen.

Allow yourself to be human. Showing strength and being there for family and friends is important. However allow yourself time to feel the emotions. Ignoring the pain you are in will not make it go away quicker. The more you ignore it the worse the pain will get until it forces you to acknowledge it. The sooner you deal with the pain of the loss the easier it will be when you are around crowds especially at the viewings and funeral services. You will still be hurting but the pain will not be magnified when you are around people. Then you will be a tower of strength for those who are still grasping what just happened.

You may think it is a sign of weakness to cry. But you can find people openly mourning in the bible. We all know the famous short verse that Jesus was found crying at the grave of Lazarus in John 11:35. Right after that the Jews surrounding him reacted to the fact Jesus was openly mourning Lazarus. *"See how he loved him"* (Jn. 11:36). Jesus was clearly bothered by what happened and took a moment to react to it. Then he raised Lazarus from the dead.

There are other examples of grief in the bible. The focus will be on David (2 Sam. 1:11, 12; and 2 Sam. 18:33). The first example of grief was in reaction to the death of Saul and Jonathan and the army that fallen. Another was in the passing of his son Absalom. Some will say that Saul and later on Absalom were a thorn in David's side. However David and Saul in their last meeting left on good terms despite being enemies. So out of respect David mourned his enemy and the people surrounding him mourned the passing of Saul at the same time. When it comes to Absalom there was not a chance to reconcile the situation. So David like Jacob (Gen. 37:32-35) was found to be in an intense form of grief. However unlike Jacob, David was brought to his senses in 2 Samuel 19:5-8.

There is another case of David handling grief that should be mentioned. Most know to some extent the events of David and Bathsheba. That resulted in a child being born, however this child did not survive. As stated in 2 Samuel 12:14 the child was going to die. Once the child was born he fell ill. David pleaded to God through fasting and lay on the ground at night (2 Sam. 12:16). But after seven days the child died. All were concerned on how David would react to the news. But David simply asked if the child died. And after getting the news he got up and carried on as he normally did. People were surprised at the turnaround. David explained he had hoped that God would have been gracious in sparing the child. But since that was not the case it was pointless to carry on thinking he could bring the child back. Does that mean that David still did not have moments of grief? He probably did. It may not be recorded in the bible how David felt afterwards, but if he is human he likely felt some pain from time to time about the loss.

There are situations where you do not expect someone to die. But in this case the result was clearly that someone was going to die. When a loved one is given news they have a few moments left to live. That creates a situation where you hope against the truth that the person is going to die. Then when it happens you are hit with numerous emotions. Some prepare for the outcome and some do not. It may feel like you are burying someone prematurely. But bracing for something that is going to happen is not a bad thing. David resolved to accept he could not save his child and moved on. He could have collapsed and broke down about the situation but he did not. How he reconciled what happened is open to debate. But we can learn from how he reacted to the news.

Initially you may not feel anything when you first hear the news of someone's passing. You may be in shock or disbelief because the reality of the news has not hit you yet. It may take a moment. Or while you are talking to others it may start sinking in what happened causing you to react to what is going on. Again do not ignore the emotions. Take a moment and go let it out. If you need to cry, scream, shout, and so on, do it. Ride out that emotion and then take a moment (or a few moments) to try and pull you together. Sadness usually comes with grief. How long will you be sad depends on how significant the loss. Just trust you won't be sad forever and eventually you find joy, peace, and happiness soon. My former priest had a saying 'for every Good Friday there is an Easter Sunday'. It may be bad now but it will get better.

You may experience anger and guilt at this time. Depending on the situation you might be angry for a variety of reasons. And may feel there was an injustice about what happened. You may feel guilt and regret about what you did or did not do. These emotions are powerful and if not dealt with can turn you inside out. When you make peace with these emotions you can gradually work to heal yourself of the pain. Forgiveness is not hard. But it does take effort. You cannot erase the memory of what happened. But you can possibly erase the sting of the pain you are in.

Fear might accompany your grief. A loss can trigger a group of concerns for you. Concerns about what may be next or how do you handle things may come up. Depending on how significant the loss was you may find yourself trying to figure out how to deal with certain responsibilities on your own. Or even concerns of your own mortality. Just remember you are not alone. After a loss you likely do not want to be bothered by people. There is only so many times you can hear "I'm sorry for your loss", and "I'm here for you", before you say enough. At these times recognize who your friends truly are that want to be there for you and let them be a means of support emotionally.

Whoever started the phrase "confession is good for the soul" was on to something. Initially when you talk about someone who passed away the conversation at first is probably about how it happened. But as you gradually start talking about what that person meant to you in life you begin to feel the joy that person gave you. And you start remembering them not just because they died but because of how they lived. Also take to heart *"For just as the sufferings of Christ are abundant for us, so also our consolation is abundant through Christ"* (2 Cor. 1:5). Jesus on his way to the cross suffered greatly. The early disciples ultimately suffered for following him. There are numerous writings in both the Old and New Testaments that discuss how to handle stressful situations. As you go through the mourning process pray on it. You know yourself better than anyone. So communication is important. Being able to express how you feel will help you overcome whatever problems you are dealing with at this time. The better you communicate things the easier it will be to move forward.

If the shoe is on the other foot you go from needing consoling to giving it. In that case the first thing you need to do is pay attention to the person. Given their ordeal it is more important that they get rid of the pain that is been draining them. The more steam they blow off the more likely the healing will begin. The more they feel there is support the better the recovery will be. What is needed is a friend who is there for them, and friends do not abandon them in need. Words of encouragement go a long way. *"Anxiety weighs down the human heart, but a good word cheers it up"* (Prov. 12:25).

Keep your ego in check. Avoid being the authority on whatever the person is experiencing. Grief is an individual experience. Even if their situation is similar to what you went through avoid putting your spin fully on their situation. If they ask then maybe offer pointers but avoid being the answer person. Consolation is not about having all the answers. It is about bearing each other's burdens and being able to support each other. If you are good friends with the person in mourning you can tell when they are starting to feel better. In conversation when the person starts talking closer to the way they normally talk and joke the pain probably is not as bad as before.

You can with patience and confidence share your faith without ramming it down someone's throat. Your thoughts and actions are a reflection of God's grace. A kind word and gesture goes a long way in helping someone.

The better you understand the situation the easier it is to share the right way words of encouragement. Just try to make sure it is not a long winded speech. *"For we are not peddlers of God's word like so many; but in Christ we speak as persons of sincerity, as persons sent from God and standing in his presence"* (2 Cor. 2:17).

Recently I had to deal with two of my Great Aunt's passing away, one on each side of the family within less than a year. My church knew about this and some were concerned about how I was holding up in the meantime. I explained that the first one was easy to deal with. The first Great Aunt to pass away was on my father's side of the family. She died just before Hurricane Sandy hit the Tri State area. And when people found I lost my aunt they avoided hurricane jokes out of sympathy. Due to the weather I could not go to work for two days. So after getting tired of watching the news coverage which seemed to repeat itself all morning, I focused on how I was feeling and resolved what had happened. After making peace with it going to the funeral was easy for me. The only hard part was the final viewing when I had to go past the front row of cousins barely holding it together which eventually made me feel something. You are not human if that scene fails to upset you to a degree. I hugged cousins and hoped for the best while walking by.

The second Great Aunt was on my mother's side. It was an awkward time. We knew things were not good for awhile. When it was clear that it was almost that time some relatives went to go see her in Georgia. My mother went that afternoon. All day I checked my phone because I know it does not take long to fly from New York to Georgia. But due to delays she did not get there until that evening. Interestingly enough I was at church that night for a funeral. After the funeral wrapped up I got a text from my mother saying she got there and it did not look good. Thankfully she got there before her aunt died. The next morning I got the call that my aunt passed. Unlike the previous situation where I had a moment to deal with it, this time I did not. However despite the scramble of work and other things the priority was to still find time to deal with those emotions before the funeral. Aside from headaches I managed the situation well at the funeral. Interestingly enough both funerals had the same sermon. In the midst of my grief, and any uneasiness I probably was feeling at the time. There was a moment of laughter that made me feel a moment of peace. Of course I covered my mouth to hide the laughter and kept it quiet so no one thought I was crazy.

A habit I got into recently when giving people sympathy cards is to include verses of encouragement. It is not an effort to ram God down anyone's throats. It is simply verses that offer comfort, encouragement, strength, and hope of peace to someone. You may not be versed in the bible but there are books sold that outline verses for many occasions to use. Use that as a sample and then when you get more into the bible, use verses you like that may offer help.

A friend of mine going through a stressful situation was telling me what was going on. After they spoke their mind I offered words of encouragement. First off saying it was ok to be uneasy about what was going on. After stating it was ok to be emotional I made a point that they should not stay in that mode. Acknowledge what they are feeling and then make peace with it. In other words be human first and then be superhuman. Allow for there to be pain and acknowledge it. Then afterwards you can be strong. There is the typical you need to be strong for others. But if you have a broken heart you are clearly a mess emotionally, mentally, and so on. Before you can be of use to anyone you need to get yourself straighten out.

After that I discussed with my friend what happened a few years ago when my Great Grandmother passed away. On my way home from work my mother called to tell me the news. After getting home I went into the bathroom and cried my eyes out for roughly an hour. After the first couple of minutes, I gradually forced out the worst of the emotions. Near the end a lot of steam was let out. The pain was still there but it was easier to make peace with what had just happened. When my father saw me at the wake before the funeral he said he was surprised how well I was holding up. I told him I was still bothered by it but dealt with the worst of the emotions.

In the end my parting advice to my friend was that whatever is bothering her that she does not hold it in. Let go as much as possible.

The pain will always be there. But the main thing is finding a way to manage it. That way you can keep going. The question always asked is when it is appropriate to resume life. There is no real answer to that. However it is important that we do continue on. There is nothing that can truly fill the void left in what you lost. But as you progress in this life you will eventually find joy, love, and happiness in due time. Take care, hold on, and trust things will get better.

Feeling sad or down about something is natural in life. But when you start having feelings of emptiness and despair that do not seem to go away that might be signs of a depression. A depression may make it hard to function and enjoy daily activities the way you normally do. It may be hard to just get through the day because of this.

Depression like all emotions is an individual experience. The situation varies depending on the person, but there are common symptoms and signs of this. It is important to note that some of these symptoms are common with normal lows in life. But the more symptoms you have that are sticking around for a while getting stronger, it is likely you are dealing with a depression. If you feel like you are falling into a hole you need to take action before it gets worse.

The greater the feelings of despair and hopelessness, the higher the possibility someone will think suicide is the only way to relieve that pain. If the situation becomes overwhelming and disabling that is a moment when you need to seek help. Signs and symptoms of depression are: feelings of helplessness and hopelessness, loss of interest in daily activities, sleep changes, anger or irritability, self loathing, reckless behavior, among other problems that may affect you mentally and physically.

There is at least one story that relates to this situation. Elijah after defeating the Priests of Baal ends up fleeing into the woods. Some consider what he went through to be along the lines of a depression. He decides to give up and hopes he dies out there in the wilderness. *"It is enough; now, O LORD, take away my life, for I am no better than my ancestors"* (1 Kings 19:4). However this wasn't the end. In a moment of calm he is awoken and told to eat something. After he eats and falls asleep, he is again awoken and told to eat something. He then ventured towards Horeb the mount of God. He spent the night in a cave.

When he was told God was going to pass by the mountain Elijah went to meet him. A great wind passed by but God was not there. Then an earthquake but God was not there. Then a fire but God was not there. Then a sound of sheer silence, Elijah found God there (1 Kings 19:11-13).

Now depending on the version of the bible you are reading that verse varies. New Revised Standard Version says God was present in sheer silence. Some versions say gentle voice and some say whisper. The general idea you should get here is that Elijah found God in a moment that is described as calm. Despite the chaos that reigned around him whether it is roaring winds, rumbling earthquakes, raging fires and so on. It is in the quiet moments when things become clear and you can focus on what needs to be done. Early on Elijah was distraught and had given up. But it was after he was sound asleep that he was woken up and given food. Whatever chaos reigns in your life, hopefully you find a moment of calm to put things in perspective.

In an extreme case, think about the book of Revelation. There are a lot of chaotic images that are recorded in the book. When it came to the seven seals the writer mentions a pause after the seventh seal was opened. *"When the Lamb opened the seventh seal, there was silence in heaven for about half an hour"* (Rev. 8:1). After reading for awhile about the things that were going on in that book, to have it on record that everything stopped for a period of time means something. Whatever rushing or busy activity you may have, take a moment. The concerns you have to take care of will always be there. But how you deal with them says more about the situation than the fact it was taken care of. When you pause for a moment and really look at the situation there is probably a better way to handle it.

Talking about peace and quiet is easy. But getting there is another story. One of the unfortunate things about being in a depression is that you are not motivated to do anything. Daily activities that would normally be routine seem hard to get done. On your own it is hard to overcome depression. And reaching out for help seems questionable at times if not overwhelming. Isolation will make what you are going through harder. Trying to maintain relationships with others is important.

Start small. When you are down and drained by depression the goal is to just get started with anything to gradually get motivated. A short walk around the block is a good way to blow off steam. You can also use a random walk to clear your head and think about things. A phone call to a friend or family member may not seem ideal. But just talking about anything will help you for a moment get your mind off what is bothering you. You do not have to tell everyone what you are going through. When you are down emotionally creating a distraction from the feelings you are dealing with is not a bad thing. You still will have to deal with what is going on. Remember that while trying to move on.

Just as in the previous chapter "Play to Your Strengths" at some point I mention making the most of your resources. Here is also where that comes into play. Take a look at the people surrounding you. Who do you feel comfortable talking to? When you are in this situation there might be feelings of, if you tell anyone what you are going through it might cause more problems for you. Finding people that are a positive influence will help you along the way. Being around people who look on the bright side of things can help out in many ways as well. The people do not necessarily have to be living successful lives. They can be people who are struggling in life but have found a way to be at peace with what they are dealing with.

There are a lot of negative thoughts in the mind of someone going through a depression. You can be harder on yourself than necessary. It is ok to criticize yourself on something you did. But know your limits on a reasonable level. Being a perfectionist is fine. Have a goal in mind to accomplish. And while you are doing that enjoy the journey. The growth you accomplish as an individual at times is more valuable than achieving the goal.

While on the road to recovery it is important to take care of your health. Make sure you regularly eat meals. Keep yourself active both physically and mentally. This means reading and on occasion exercising. Elijah at first was awoken to eat food. He ate enough to walk for a lengthy period of time. In 1 Kings 19:8 it is said after eating he walked for forty days and nights. Elijah after first giving up was gradually brought back from the edge. Overcoming depression is not easy. But it is possible. The desire for change has to happen first. When you are sick of feeling the way you do that is where it starts. Then gradual steps will take place. Do not be discouraged by setbacks. Change is never instant. Take whatever disappointments may come and keep moving forward. Set a goal of what you want to change as you come out of your situation. And enjoy the journey. What change occurs with you on the journey is just as important as the journey itself.

Depression like other feelings of hopelessness if not managed right could lead to thoughts and acts of suicide. There are examples of suicide in the bible. The ones that come to mind are King Saul in 1 Samuel 31:4, Judas in Matthew 27:3-5, and the Jailer of Paul and Silas in Acts 16:27-30. Well actually two were suicides and one was a near suicide. Again I will repeat the verse used in the previous chapter of this book: *"For godly grief produces a repentance that leads to salvation and brings no regret, but worldly grief produces death"* (2 Cor. 7:10).

In the case of King Saul he was surrounded by the Philistines in battle. They were losing badly and were about to be captured. Saul asked his armor bearer to kill him with the sword. But he refused. So Saul threw himself on a sword killing him. Saul probably felt a strong sense of abandonment. An army was closing in on him with no aid in sight. There was likely a strong sense of hopelessness and doom surrounding him. He ultimately chose to die instead of leaving his fate in the hands of his enemies. In the heat of the situation it is open to debate how anyone would react. However despite how desperate and hopeless the situation might be never lose hope. Maintain your faith. Somewhere and somehow things will work out. But if you give up you will never know.

In the case of Judas he felt guilty for betraying Jesus. He tried to correct what he did wrong by first repenting then returning the money he was paid. Those who he spoke to in trying to correct the situation didn't listen. In the end Judas hung himself from a tree. Judas may have been encouraged to betray Jesus for money. However when it dawned on him what he did for money, the guilt probably outweighed the payday. Judas to his credit tried to correct what he did wrong. Unfortunately he did not stay the course. When he failed to correct what he did he killed himself. You cannot undo past regrets. But you can choose not to continue doing those actions. Repentance is turning away from what you did wrong in the past. Some people will still remind you of what you did. Leave it alone. Forgive yourself and make peace with what you did. Then make a solid effort to carry yourself in a way that shows you are no longer involved in that activity.

When it comes to the Jailer of Paul and Silas that story has a happy ending. Paul and Silas were: attacked, stripped, beaten with rods, flogged, imprisoned, and then were locked in stocks as is stated in Acts 16:22-24. When midnight came instead of despair coming from Paul and Silas about their situation, they were actually praying and singing while the prisoners listened. There was an earthquake that shook the prison and opened all the doors. The jailer thought all the prisoners escaped. Feeling guilty about what probably happened he drew his sword to kill himself in shame. *But Paul shouted in a loud voice, "Do not harm yourself, for we are all here"* (Acts 16:28). When the jailer checked it out he realized things were actually ok. Following that he asked what he needed to do. And he followed through with taking the necessary steps.

There will be periods where you will feel desperate, alone and overwhelmed by things. Saying it is wrong to feel that way is a lie. However in those times never give up. Saul and Judas gave up and it ended badly for them. The jailer could have given up but he didn't. Someone assured him things were ok when he thought he failed and it was hopeless. You may not have someone right a way to help you. But there is always a helping hand somewhere waiting for you. It may not be obvious but it is there if you look without judgment. Take heart and stay strong. Things will work out if you do not completely give into despair. *"No testing has overtaken you that is not common to everyone. God is faithful, and he will not let you be tested beyond your strength, but with the testing he will also provide the way out so that you may be able to endure it"* (1 Cor. 10:13).

There is nothing like a betrayal of trust. *"Many proclaim themselves loyal, but who can find one worthy of trust"* (Prov. 20:6). Betrayal can come from either a friend or family member. In situations like this it is not always easy to tell who you should trust. And it may be hard to tell who your friends are. Before you think that all people are out to get you, take heart that it is not the case. For the most part people are trying to live honest lives. Things happen and the outcomes become what they are. However despite whatever has happened avoid giving up on people. And please avoid the motto 'trust no one'. Take an honest look at what happened. Look at what both sides did wrong. Pray on it. See what the bible says about friendship. *"Some friends play at friendship but a true friend sticks closer than one's nearest kin"* (Prov. 18:24). Learn how to better pick your friends to help you along your way and understand the mistakes of the past. Grow from it. Not everyone is a friend. Also not everyone is an enemy.

When Jesus was betrayed by Judas, Jesus says to him *"Friend, do what you are here to do"* (Matt. 26:50). It can be debated what really caused Judas to betray Jesus. This is will not be discussed here. What will be discussed is the behavior of Jesus in this situation. As many of you know Judas betrayed Jesus which led to Jesus being arrested and ultimately crucified. In Matthew's account when Jesus is arrested he calls Judas 'friend'. He never says anything angry or hurtful.

"See, this alone I found, that God made human beings straightforward, but they have devised many schemes" (Eccl. 7:29). There are decent people out there and there are those who do you harm. It is not always easy to tell who is really there for you. In time hopefully you will be able to open up and not worry about being hurt the way you were before. No one

gets by completely on their own unless they live a hermit like existence. Friendships like all relationships are an individual experience. So make the most of them. *"Two are better than one, because they have a good reward for their toil. For if they fall, one will lift up the other; but woe to one who is alone and falls and does not have another to help"* (Eccl. 4:9, 10).

Along with betrayal let us not forget about bullying. *"You know the insults I receive, and my shame and dishonor; my foes are all known to you. Insults have broken my heart, so that I am in despair. I looked for pity, but there was none; and for comforters, but I found none"* (Ps. 69: 19, 20). Bullying can take on various forms in life. Growing up there were many situations where someone pushed and bothered me. What I dealt with growing up is not nearly as bad as what goes on today. Bullying took on a number of forms whether it was teasing. The spreading of rumors that was not true about someone. Leaving people out on purpose when involved in certain activities. As well as being attacked physically.

In my case it was either a problem at school or in the neighborhood. These days it is much more magnified since there are numerous outlets for expression. Internet was not as widely used then as it is today. If I had a bad day there was some privacy. Now because of social media it is easy to spread bad news about someone anywhere. When you are bullied it is not an easy situation to deal with at times. However give it time and things will work out.

The unfortunate case with all bullying is that people who experience it end up feeling alone, unpopular, powerless among other feelings. While discussing bullying with a group of Acolytes during a meeting I stressed a few things. First off tell your parents or an adult you were the victim of bullying. Sometimes with the way people play around it is not always easy to tell something happened. It is important that they do not keep the situation to themselves. The sooner they open up about what occurred. The sooner it could be resolved. In these cases help will come in resolving a problem personally. In the case of cyber bullying that is a different situation. People are hurling insults from a distance. Whether it is true what they are saying or not, have the strength and courage to take what is being said. Stay true to yourself and the truth will come out soon enough.

In both the Old and New Testaments there are at times antagonistic relationships. In the book of Judges you see the people being oppressed and after a period of time someone called a Judge came to their aid. The Judge was to an extent a Freedom Fighter. The Judge would lead the people out of the trouble.

You have Othiniel liberating the people from King Cushan-rishathaim of Aram-naharaim in Judges 3:7-11. Ehud liberating the people from King Eglon of Moab in Judges 3:12-30. Shamgar fighting the Philistines in Judges 3:31. Deborah with Barak called to lead the way against King Jabin of Canaan in Judges 4. Gideon called to aid in fighting against the Midianites and Amalekites in Judges 7, 8. Jephthah called to aid in fighting the Ammonites in Judges 11:4-33. And Samson called to fight against the Philistines in Judges 13-16.

In these instances you see people in trouble calling for aid and receiving it. Steps were taken to get help. It did not come right away. But it came. When you are in trouble it is easy to be impatient waiting for help to come. Trust that help will come and the solutions may or may not be clear.

Know when to pick your battles the right way. Sometimes you don't really have to fight someone to win a battle. You are familiar with the example I gave of Elisha in the previous chapter. Elisha while aiding against the King of Aram managed to bring about peace without fighting. Along with that story, think about David when he was pursued by Saul. In 1 Samuel 18:7-12 you find that Saul grew jealous of David and tried to kill him. Over the next few chapters you see David making his escape from Saul. There are two accounts in 1 Samuel 24 and 26 where Saul is unknowingly at David's mercy however David spares the life of Saul. In both exchanges when Saul realizes what happened both leave each other with a level of respect. There will be times where someone you have an antagonistic relationship will be at your mercy. That is not the time to have a cocky attitude. If you follow the greatest commandment that means loving everyone, with that said love your enemies as well as your friends. Choose wisely when to fight and when not to. Sometimes an act of kindness goes a long way into winning a battle. No *"if your enemies are hungry, feed them; if they are thirsty, give them something to drink; for by doing this you will heap burning coals on their heads"* (Rom. 12:20).

In the New Testament you find the early Disciples dealing with on occasion persecutions. In John 20:19 you find the disciples in hiding following the death of Jesus. When you get to the book of Acts you find at times the disciples arrested (Acts 4:3; 5:18; 12:3; 16:23; 21:33), flogged (Acts 5:40), and sometimes killed (Acts 7:58; 12:2) for what they were doing. Whatever struggles you are dealing with physically, mentally, spiritually. I hope you find help, support, and peace in what you are going through. *"I consider that the sufferings of this present time are not worth comparing with the glory about to be revealed to us"* (Rom. 8:18).

When a situation arises try and keep a cool head regardless of what is going on. Have a moment of anguish but remain prayerful and patient. *"Answer me when I call, O God of my right! You gave me room when I was in distress. Be gracious to me, and hear my prayer"* (Psalm 4:1). And even if the situation makes you restless do what you can to take care of yourself. If God rested so can you. *"When you are disturbed, do not sin; ponder it on your beds, and be silent. I will lie down and sleep in peace; for you alone, O LORD, make me lie down in safety"* (Ps. 4:4, 8).

The saying "Let go and Let God", and the song "I surrender all" does not work if you are carrying any type of baggage, burden, issues, and so on. Regardless of whatever distractions and excuses you make to avoid a situation, you still need to confront the issues bothering you. When you honestly deal with whatever is bothering you. That is when the healing can truly begin and you are able to move on carrying the burden you are dealing with.

The Psalms teach us a lot about prayer. The Psalms vary depending on the situation. They show a people speaking to God in a number of ways. For this particular chapter the focus will be on Psalms that focus on being in trouble, despair, and trying to find peace. They may start from a bad point sometimes. But the ending is usually hopeful. When we are suffering we begin from a low point at times. However things do not have to end there. We can in time end up in a better situation.

For example Psalm 25 is about Guidance and Deliverance. *"Turn to me and be gracious to me, for I am lonely and afflicted"* (Ps. 25:16). Over the course of reading that Psalm you come across the basics of praying for help. The Psalmist believed is crying out to God putting his trust in him. In God he will not know any shame. He asks for God to show him the way. He asks God to be merciful on past mistakes. After explaining the benefits of following the path of God's guidance, the Psalm concludes with a plea for help from the troubles surrounding the Psalmist.

Psalm 73 is an example of a plea for relief from those who oppress you. *"My flesh and my heart may fail, but God is the strength of my heart and my portion forever"* (Ps. 73:26). It deals to a degree with struggle. The Psalmist starts out with mentioning how they believe God is good to those who are just. Then it launches into issues with people who are not that way. Afterwards it states that despite what surrounds him the Psalmist will remain true the path God guides him towards. And in the end believes that being near to God is a good thing.

Psalm 32 talks about the benefits of forgiveness. When you use the power of forgiveness you feel a release from whatever pain you were dealing with. The Psalm begins stating how carefree people are when they are forgiven. Then points out how when you are weighed down it is a burden. But when you acknowledge what you did wrong and make an effort to correct it the healing process will begin. *"Happy are those whose transgression is forgiven, whose sin is covered"* (Ps. 32:1).

There are at least two Psalms that appear not to have a happy ending which are Psalms 44 and 58. In Psalm 44 in the beginning of the Psalm the writer discusses the distant past of what God did for them. But as the Psalm progresses it seems that the prayers and faith in God have produced no results. Both help and hope might seem distant. However it is there. Just hold on and try to be patient. *"Why do you hide your face? Why do you forget our affliction and oppression"* (Ps. 44:24).

Psalm 58 is by no means a model prayer for you to use. The plea for vengeance goes to the point of wishing bad things on others. It is a far cry from the call to love your enemies. There is nothing wrong with being angry or disturbed. However you should not act on those feelings. Seeking revenge is never a good thing. *"O God, break the teeth in their mouths; tear out the fangs of the young lions, O LORD"* (Ps. 58:6).

While in an emotional state you will likely say and be tempted to do things that are hurtful to others. But wishing doom on others is not a good thing. As angry as the 58 Psalm seems at times. Do your best not to follow that example. *"Be angry but do not sin; do not let the sun go down on your anger, and do not make room for the devil"* (Eph. 4:26, 27).

While staying with Psalms there is one that discusses how God was a calming influence for his people. Psalm 107 shows a number of situations where God saves his people from trouble. There are roughly four accounts of God delivering his people from a bad situation. In one account of the people being in trouble God displayed his power by being a calming influence. *"Then they cried to the LORD in their trouble, and he brought them out from their distress; he made the storm be still, and the waves of the sea were hushed. Then they were glad because they had quiet, and he brought them to their desired haven"* (Ps. 107:28-30).

In the Gospel accounts it is said that Jesus stills a storm. Matthew, Mark, and Luke all give a telling of this story. There are slight differences in some of the telling but all agree Jesus and the Disciples enter the boat to cross the sea and are suddenly overwhelmed by a storm that appears and causes much panic. Jesus then stands up and calms the storm amazing his followers and they are on their way. Of the three Gospels only Mark records what Jesus was saying while he calmed the storm. *"Peace! Be still"* (Mk. 4:39).

Both the Psalm and the text from the Gospel give reference to God being a comfort to you. However you need to know how to approach that. Being in pain is normal when something bad happens. You can be broken down mentally, physically, as well as spiritually. The pain can possibly be so bad you are unable to accept any help offered at that time. Just know that help is there. And when you are ready it will be also.

Just as previously when discussing bullying help came in some form or another, as people of faith when seeking help in time of trouble help will come. Whatever grief and despair you are struggling with you are never truly alone in your pain. Friends come and go. But the constant we have is our faith in God. And God will send help to aid you in your time of trouble. Some help will be easily recognized and some won't be. But it will come if you look and pay attention. In Psalm 107 you read how God delivered people out of whatever trouble they were in. In the Gospel account you see Jesus calming the fears of his followers.

This chapter touched on a few general situations that you may encounter from time to time. There is no absolute solution to prevent any of it from happening. But there are a number of ways you can deal with it so that it is bearable. During the storms raging around you, hopefully you find the much needed comfort, support, strength, confidence, courage, and above all peace in your situation. *"Come to me, all you that are weary and are carrying heavy burdens, and I will give you rest. Take my yoke upon you, and learn from me; for I am gentle and humble in heart, and you will find rest for your souls. For my yoke is easy, and my burden is light"* (Matt. 11:28-30).

There is a popular story called "Footprints" where a person is walking on the beach with God. At first there were two sets of footprints. But at some point there was only one set. The person looking back noticed it and asked God why there was only one set. And God answered when the person was carrying a burden, God carried them.

There was another story where a person carrying a cross felt it was too heavy for them to carry. So they asked to change crosses for a lighter one. After trying out all the crosses they found one that was just right. Turned out the one that seemed too heavy to carry was the one that suited them in the end.

When seeking help in time of trouble keep your options open to the resources available to you. In your struggles there are numerous forms of counseling you can go to. It may seem awkward to do it but humbling yourself to admit you need help will allow you to be able to seek help better. When you understand better who is really there to help you it will be easier to rely on them for help. Pray on it. If you aren't sure how to do it look to the Psalms listed as possible guides to figure out the right way to pray. There are hints out there on how to go about things if you take the time to look. Make sure you are honestly trying to resolve a situation. Some may turn to drinking among other things to help cope with situations. But that is just a temporary fix. The emotions and pain you are dealing with will still be waiting for you. Until you confront the situation it will always be there waiting to bother you.

As a child or teenager you are a minor. Sometimes to get the required help might rely on parent or legal guardian consent. Once you identify what is wrong, do what you can to communicate to them what is bothering you so the necessary steps can be taken. Adults can only guess what is wrong. But they will not know for certain what is bothering you if you fail to communicate with them. Along with seeking help do not forget about the comforting aspects of your faith. Focusing on areas that produce encouragement, support, and comfort will help with the healing aspects of your situation.

Whatever trial you endured do not think you are out of the woods completely. When Jesus was tempted in the wilderness the Gospel of Luke records the following: *"When the devil had finished every test, he departed from him until an opportune time"* (Lk. 4:13). With that said it means that the encounters with the devil did not end here. Jesus would likely have to deal with other challenges from the devil.

Throughout the Gospels there are a number of accounts of Jesus casting out demons and curing the sick. In Luke 11:24-26 there is telling of an unclean spirit returning. After an unclean spirit leaves it wanders for a time then comes back to haunt the person it left worse than before. Whatever bad elements we dealt with before, we cannot fully rejoice in beating them. We need to stay vigilant and take steps to avoid whatever bad elements surrounding us the first time may try to take hold a second time. Understand how you got into the mess you were in. And take steps so that you do not fall so deep into it and end up worse than before.

There was plenty of discussion about difficult situations in this chapter. The topics were discussed as general as possible since each experience is individual and varies to an extent. Whatever situation you find yourself in make sure you seek help in dealing with it. As well as take care of your health. There is a saying and a song that goes eyes are the soul. Luke 11:34 says: *"Your eye is the lamp of your body. If your eye is healthy, your whole body is full of light; but if it is not healthy, your body is full of darkness."* You are never the same let alone 100% after a wound. There are assumed timetables for recovery from physical, emotional, mental, spiritual, etc. wounds. It all depends on the individual. Recovery depends more on how you choose to live with the wound. The better you deal with the problem the better off you will be.

There is a Gospel account of Jesus visited Mary and Martha in Luke 10:38-42. You see two different personalities at work here. The story goes that Mary was attentive to Jesus while Martha busied herself with housework. When situations come up we tend to be more like Martha as opposed to Mary. Martha was preoccupied with the housework. In general there will always be work to do in life. So being Martha is at times necessary. However do not be preoccupied with daily activities to the point where you fail to take care of your needs as an individual. In this case Mary chose to focus on the matter at hand which was the visitor Jesus. If God rested so can you. Take a moment during your scrambling around to refresh yourself. You never know how tired you really are until you are not actively moving around. The same way you focus on getting tasks done, take a moment and focus on recharging yourself.

Early on when discussing inadequacies I brought up how some of the leaders that appear in the bible struggled with theirs. *"If any of you is lacking in wisdom, ask God, who gives to all generously and ungrudgingly, and it will be given you"* (Jam. 1:5). The book of James is very straightforward in discussing a variety of issues. In the following verses James 1:2-7 he addresses how to face trials and challenges. Whenever challenges come to test you it allows you to grow as an individual. And along with discussing individual growth he also mentions how to approach God for help. In whatever situations you face in life try to face it in a calm manner. And honestly deal with it so the problems won't add up later on. Stay strong, stay safe, and be careful. *"Rejoice in hope, be patient in suffering, persevere in prayer"* (Rom. 12:12).

CHAPTER SIX

To the Future

"He must increase, but I must decrease" (Jn. 3:30).

Here we are at last. A lot of things have been discussed here. And it has all built up to this moment. The text when read within the Gospel of John shows a transition from people following John the Baptist to now starting to follow Jesus. When John's followers notice the change he makes that statement. John figuratively passed the torch to Jesus. There are other areas in the bible where you see a transition of leadership. Along with Jesus passing the torch to the disciples, you also have Elijah and Elisha, King David and King Solomon, Paul to Timothy, as well as Moses to Joshua.

Transition periods are always interesting. And can possibly be emotional. For both sides it is the end of a certain journey. For a mentor you spend a moment devoting time to training and preparing someone. After awhile it comes a time where you realize you did all you could to prepare them. As a protégé you invest time in learning all you can about a particular situation. Then you get to the point of graduation. There is only so much time that can be spent in preparation. After awhile it is all about carrying out what you learned as best as you can.

It is interesting to think of what possibly went through the minds of leaders when their time drew to a close and it came to that moment to say to their successors it is time. When it came to that moment where Moses was going to leave his people, what emotions filled his mind. This was his life and now it was time to go. What thoughts filled the people who followed him as well as Joshua as they inherited the legacy of Moses? What thoughts filled Elijah's mind when he left Elisha? And so on. The imagination runs wild thinking of what thoughts filled the minds of people that passed the torch and received the torch.

For example Moses liberated his people. And he led them through the wilderness for decades before they entered the Promised Land. However as you know Moses wasn't allowed to enter the land it is detailed in Numbers 20:12. After he addressed his people for the last time and passed the torch to his successor Joshua in the book of Deuteronomy. The formal passing of the torch from Moses to Joshua happens in Numbers 27:12-23.

By the time of the book of the Deuteronomy it was the final moments of Moses with his people. Given that this was to be his final address it was important to say all he could possibly say. With that he reminded them of their history. He went over various instructions on how they should carry themselves. And then he made closing remarks before his death. He did all he could do to prepare them for what is to come. Now it was time for them to carry on. Moses would not lead them into the Promised Land and ultimately settle there. Unlike the grumbling that accompanied Moses during the Exodus. During the time of Joshua things were calm. Joshua only had to deal with two tasks: launch a military campaign to take control of the land God promised, and then parcel out the conquered land among the tribes. What Moses started Joshua completed.

The events involving Solomon succeeding his father David was touched on briefly in the fourth chapter of this book. David while near death named Solomon as his successor who would rule the kingdom of Israel. After David fought many battles on behalf of his people,

Solomon would go on to rule in a period of peace. Because of the blood on David's hands due to the numerous battles he fought it would be up to Solomon to build the temple for God (1 Chr. 28).

As the transition period went on David charged Solomon with being faithful to following and serving God. During that time David left instructions on how to follow God and what needed to be done. Following the death of King David, Solomon would take over as king. After establishing his rule as king, Solomon prayed to God for wisdom to rule (1 Kings 3:6-9). As long as Solomon followed God the way his father David instructed he prospered. And the kingdom saw joy as Solomon succeeded in building the temple of God. The torch passed successfully from father to son. For the remainder of the time Solomon reigned as king the nation prospered.

Not much is known about the tutelage Elisha received from Elijah. We do know when Elijah met Elisha (1 Kings 19:19-21), and when Elijah left Elisha (2 Kings 2:1-12). We can piece together their relationship to an extent. Three times Elijah would say he is going somewhere to Elisha, Elisha would say he will not leave Elijah (2 Kings 2:2; 2:4; 2:6). And every time that exchange took place an added conversation would happen. The company of prophets would say to Elisha that the LORD was taking away his master, only for Elisha to say he knew and for them to keep silent (2 Kings 2:3; 2:5).

When it came time to part ways there was one more mentor/protégé moment. Elijah had one last conversation with Elisha. Since this was the last time they would see each other Elijah asked if there were any final requests. Elisha asked for a double share of Elijah's spirit (2 Kings 2:9). Elijah said it was difficult request to grant. But he would do it if Elisha met a certain condition. After Elijah left, Elisha received the mantle that was Elijah's. Elisha's wish was granted of the double share. There are more details of the deeds and works of Elisha than there is of Elijah.

There are times when it can be a challenge. We see in parts of the Gospels when the focus turned to Jesus teaching his Disciples. The moments vary from the Disciples learning lessons from Jesus, to at times Jesus being frustrated with how they didn't understand what he was telling them. In the end after the resurrection the Disciples were well on their way.

When thinking of those situations I have been on both ends of the spectrum. In my lifetime I have been in the situation where someone tapped me to take over where they left off. And I also have stepped down and left things in someone else's hands. It is hard to say which situation was hardest for me. Succeeding someone is a daunting task. And naming a successor is also difficult too. I have also been witness to a passing of torches as well. Since this is a church publication the focus will be on situations within the church.

Along with some biblical figures some real life situations come to mind when it comes to a passing the torch. Immediately what comes to mind is when my predecessor who ran the Acolytes broke the news that he was stepping down as head of the group and tapping me to take over. For years we worked together leading the group.

The situation was interesting because around the time I had just pulled myself together after personal tragedy led to another depression. After coming through that it led to me speaking on Youth Sunday at church. That day I did a sermon based on John 21: 15-17. The joy I had in the success of that day immediately turned to doom. It was the end of an era. Personally I knew it was going to happen one of these days but nothing ever really prepares you for that moment when it does happen. It was a shocker and while telling my mother what happened I had a doomed look on my face. As you found out in the first chapter of this book when I took over as head of the Acolytes some time later I became Verger. No one in the history of my church ever did that. That makes my situation unique among previous leaders of the Acolytes. My predecessor was there to cheer me on during the ceremony and gave me encouragement in the next stage of my journey.

Recently the in my Diocese the Bishop of New York announced his retirement. Mark Sisk who served my Diocese as Bishop was leaving us. That began the process of electing a new Bishop. With that said the

Diocese gathered to elect a Bishop Coadjutor to succeed the outgoing Bishop. One of the acolytes of my church asked me what that process meant. So my explanation was George W. Bush was the President of the United States. Barack Obama was the President Elect. When George W. Bush's term expired Barack Obama would be sworn in as President. The Bishop Coadjutor is similar to the President Elect so after the current Bishop leaves the Bishop Coadjutor would be sworn in as the next Bishop.

On the day of the elections where local churches gathered with representatives involved in the election process. There was a simple service that day and after that would begin the election process. The candidates would be presented to the crowd gathered and testimonies given on behalf of them. The candidate would have to win a certain amount of votes from both clergy and lay members. This would take a few rounds. After each round there was a caucus where candidates and supporters would try to win support from others to get more votes. After the election process the Bishop Coadjutor was picked. Following that the transition period of the Bishop Coadjutor taking over as Bishop began. There was a farewell service for the outgoing Bishop and then a formal installation of the incoming Bishop. At the end of the formal ceremony of Installation, Bishop Sisk would hand Bishop Dietsche the Crozier which is the staff of office for Bishop.

In this case the one elected as the Bishop Coadjutor was Andrew Dietsche who I saw several times alongside Bishop Sisk as a Bishop Chaplain. A Bishop Chaplain assists the Bishop during visits to events. Since the two worked together to an extent it wasn't much of a transition period where Bishop Dietsche had to get familiar with the area and environment he would be working in. The Diocese already knew him.

The situations listed features a torched being passed to a successor in various ways. Moses dies sometime after naming his successor Joshua. David is dying and names Solomon his successor. Elijah after training Elisha is taken to heaven. Jesus after a time with his disciples leaves them to carry on. However not all the situations I mention involve someone dying. When I succeeded my predecessor he was not dying. And to this day we still talk to each other. In regards to the Bishop situation, no one was dying. I have not stepped down from any positions recently but as a mentor the role of teaching and encouraging is still going on.

"The student is not above the teacher, but everyone who is fully trained will be like their teacher" (Lk. 6:40 NIV). There is a unique bond that forms between teachers/or mentors and students/or protégé's. There is the formal one that is in a relationship. Then depending on the moment the bonds can lead to friendship that is near to family ties. When someone is following behind a person learning from them, the goal is to be on their level of understanding at some point.

There is a saying that a teacher loves to see their students surpass them. However is a student ever greater than their teacher? That is open to debate. The journey a person takes is an individual one. Whenever I am in a situation of succeeding someone, I worry less about being like them and matching what they did. And focus more on being myself and doing the best job I can. In the end is it my journey not theirs. Just as the path you take is up to you.

When it comes to the relationship with my protégé it is interesting. When he joined the Acolytes he was told that the Verger leads the group. He was curious to know what a Verger was. After meeting me he asked what it took to be become a Verger, and I told him just listen to everything I say. From then on he asked plenty of questions and took after me in many ways. Over time along with training him as an Acolyte, there were moments where he asked for advice on a variety of topics.

Long story short, when it came time for his High School Graduation I felt it was important to give him a few words of wisdom to help guide him through the rigors of college life. Knowing him he likely has a copy of this book you are reading. With that said he probably recognized some of the verses I gave him in his graduation card appearing in the first chapter of this book. The motivation for the verses came from the tone of the one of the letters Paul wrote to Timothy. In 2 Timothy, Paul is figuratively passing the torch to Timothy.

In the letter you see the bonds of a teacher and a student. Paul greets Timothy warmly and reflects on their relationship. Then proceeds to encourage and instruct Timothy. Just as Jesus commissioned his Disciples, Paul figuratively commissions Timothy *"As for you, always be sober, endure suffering, do the work of an evangelist, carry out your ministry fully"* (2 Tim. 4:5).

My protégé was not going away for college however he was probably going to be rather busy so we would not meet as often as before. With that said it was important to give him a decent parting shot, where he had something to carry him through potentially rough times. There is only so much time you can spend in preparation. After awhile what needs to be executed has to take place.

There have been a variety of things covered in this book. My former mentor when giving me an idea for a book suggested writing an inspirational book for the youth. With that I began writing with the idea of doing a book that helped guide individuals to not only approach thinking on their own, but help them figure out how to deal with certain things while growing as an individual. The goal was to plant a seed as it were in the reader giving them some ideas on how to approach things.

That is what drove my approach to this chapter. A lot has been said and discussed over the last few chapters. The goal was to give you ideas on how to approach and deal with certain things. Trends come and go so talking about technological advances now may seem dated within a few years. However human nature has not changed over the centuries. So giving basic practical advice was the goal here. All that you read here was planning and preparation on a basic level. After you find a structure that works for you then, you can move on to do what needs to be done.

Following the Introduction the remaining chapters branched off from the first one which was a general response to "Calling". We get called for a variety of things: a call to lead, a call to serve, along with a host of other situations. The purpose of that chapter was to examine how to react to being called on for something. As stated in the chapter it is easy to give up and say you are not up to the challenge.

However when you examine the call of others, you find there are plenty of stories similar to your situation. Calling is never convenient. Most probably are not planning to do anything heroic or spectacular when they receive the calling for anything. Before throwing your hands up and quitting before starting. Take an honest look at who you are and what you are capable of.

While you are examining the type of person you are eliminate all excuses you may have about why you are not up to the task at hand. In examining that find out where you are skilled at and where you need help. When you understand that, building a team to help you achieve the goals needed to be successful will become easier.

When you understand what is needed. Then you can start evaluating what you really need and then go from there. You may not have all the resources needed at the time but that is where team building comes into place. The team compliments what you are trying to accomplish. Building a team to succeed in what you are trying to do will take time. There is no real time limit on success. There is a time limit on executing the things you have planned.

Basic skills involved in team building are: planning, communication, and cooperation. There is only so much time you can spend talking about the plan. If all you are doing is meeting up and talking but nothing is getting done. Time to an extent is being wasted. Setting long range and short range goals will go a long way in terms of realizing goals moving forward.

Having a vision and being able to communicate that to others is important. In learning to work with others you need to be able to talk honestly with them. Being able to talk to groups of people is not easy. And no matter how seasoned someone is in speaking there is still a level of challenge. Being "Politically Correct" does not prevent you from completely being offensive to someone. Making an effort to understand where a person is coming from and allowing them to know you as a person will make communication easy for all.

When I started working at my current job the Floor Manager at the time said during the interview process that there are a lot of characters here. If something is a problem bring it to him. The first few weeks at the job were a feeling out process. Learning what is expected of me, all the while getting used to my coworkers. Once I understood where they were coming from there was less friction while working there.

Working in a group setting can be both a joy and challenge. You will either get along with the people you are dealing with, or have problems with them. During the third chapter of this book I mention two situations involving me in a group setting. One was a joy and another was frustrating.

In a perfect world there would be no problems with people. But unfortunately there will cases where problems exist. Some can be resolved and some cannot. Do not let bad experiences discourage you. Learn from them and move on. Not everyone is a villain. Make sure you know what you are trying to do and what you bring to the table. When you understand that it is easy to find your voice and where you fit in. At my previous job I was asked how I could put up with certain people. My response was I do not have to like you to work with you. I just have to work with you. And when I left the job it was not hard to put the situations that caused me grief behind me.

In one situation in this book I mentioned one person that was in charge was very rough and demanding. The mistake he made was trying to do all the planning in one day. The event had a lot of variables and he did not make the most of his resources. Given that I knew who was around me and what I would likely have to deal with. I already planned out how to deal with things and keep myself fresh for the majority of that day in case something came up. And since not everything was planned out it was a good thing having the approach I did have.

When you are in charge of something you may be empowered to deal with a variety of things. And with that comes pressure to get it right. However avoid being a jerk when doing things. Create an environment where people understand it is all on you. But make it a collaborative effort. The more you work with people the easier the task becomes. Have a plan on how to get things done. And be open to ideas from others. There might be a situation where someone has an idea that compliments or makes your plan better.

When involved with events elsewhere for example my involvement at the cathedral. There is a meeting to plan out things and the organizers know who can make it and who is tied up somewhere. So all the planning is not done at that meeting. They meet with who is there and plan out the more complicated stuff then. And when all are gathered the day of the event, the remaining assignments are given out during the meeting beforehand. The success of the event depends on how well you communicate with others.

If you are in charge people will follow you. That is as long as you act like you know what you are talking about. And if the instructions you are giving are clear and understandable. But if after a walkthrough of a plan people are still confused and have questions there will be problems and people will not want to work with you. Make sure you know the material enough to tell people what they need to know so they are able to help you get the job done. When you do that properly people will always respect you.

On the other hand if you are following behind someone and playing a role supporting someone make sure you understand what they need from you. When possible attend the meetings given so you know what needs to be taken care of. In finding out what they need from you learn how they would like you to approach doing something. The more in sync you are with what they are doing the easier things will be for both. Working with others is a challenge, but at times can be rewarding.

The third chapter was a clearly a continuation of the first chapter. During the course of the second chapter of this book was a discussion on finding your voice. While the first half was about finding your voice and learning how to speak in public. The second half was about getting into the bible.

Communication was discussed on a basic level in the third chapter. However the need to learn how to find your voice needed to be discussed in a little better detail. Knowing how to talk to people is a honed skill.

And you need to work on that occasionally. How you talk to friends is not always the way you talk to others. With that said you need to take a moment and learn how to communicate with others to avoid problems.

After discussing learning how to speak and when the best possible time to say something is, it felt natural to conclude with discussing the bible. The discussion concerning the bible was meant to be basic in nature. There is a lot of information on using the bible and how it was put together. We are exposed to bits of it when we attend church services. However in getting into using it that is another story. With that said I attempted to explore certain aspects of it. Hopefully that makes it easier to approach the bible.

The first three chapters were about for the most part skill development. The fourth chapter was about who you are as a person and the choices you make. When it comes to discussions about beliefs it can be challenging because of potential clashing. Personally I dislike those discussions and worry whether or not my comments are appropriate.

The beginning part of the chapter discussed how to follow God. Over the course of the chapter there was an attempt to explain how to approach following God and examples were given on how to do it. Any experience you have following God is an individual one. People help provide a structure on what to do as well as how to approach things. But it is and always will be, up to you what happens next.

There are a number of influences out there that can provide a number of messages both good and bad for you. Television, music, and any other form of entertainment provide a message. When you understand the type of person you want to be, then figuring out what the potential path you want to take will be made easier. Knowing who you are and where you want to go gives you a direction in life.

Your life will see good moments and bad moments. Environment provides a host of situations that may be helpful or harmful to you. At times you could be caught up in whatever is going on at the time. Just remember it is not how you start it is how you finish. Things might not be ideal or great now. But with effort and patience things will get better. People and circumstances play a part in what happens to you. Just remember regardless of what is going on you still play some part in what went on. You are responsible for your own actions. The decisions you make past and present have a role in the events that happen to you next. Make sure whatever you decide is something you can live with.

You may not have a great personal history but it does not matter what did happen. If you made the choice to turn away from what was going on and pursue doing right by yourself and others. Then stick to it. People will always talk about what bad things you used to do. Just remember it is talk. You no longer are involved in questionable activities there is nothing to worry about except continuing to do what is right for you and others.

Race issues will always exist in some form or another. When I mentioned about Martin Luther King Jr. it was not an attempt to bring on any guilt trips to other races. The Civil Rights Movement brought about a variety of changes that affected how things were done in the country. Segregation was no longer that blatant afterwards. While talking about that in this book my concern was to avoid attacking anyone. I was not even born when that went on. But in reading about what had happened and understanding what my parent's generation and earlier generations dealt with. It made me appreciate more what someone like a Martin Luther King Jr. and countless others went through and sacrificed for my benefit.

When Barack Obama was running for President there were a number of references to Martin Luther King Jr. so I made an effort to bridge the gap and explain how things changed over the decades. I was not trying to make Barack Obama out to be a great man. History will ultimately decide where he stands as a person.

One of the unfortunate parts of the history of our country is the involvement in Slavery. Racism is a major issue in the country. Slavery unfortunately is a touchy subject that is not easily discussed. It becomes harder when someone brings up the fact that slavery appears in the bible. Being black and justifying being Christian when discussions turn to that is challenging. Trying to rationalize that is hard. The only thing that can be said is that if you choose to be involved in a church and follow the Christian faith it is by choice. The Christian faith was not forced on you in this day and age. Hopefully you were not brainwashed into following the beliefs concerning Christians.

Aside from that whichever church you are affiliated with do not hold a bias to another church. If Jesus told his disciples not to hold anything against someone not part of their group, you should not do it either. As long as they share the same core of beliefs as a Christian that you have leave it alone. It they are not welcoming to you ignore them. No one is perfect so there is no perfect church. We are in this together.

As stated before my mentor urged me to write an inspirational book for the youth. However in writing on ideas of how to approach interacting with others as well as developing who you are as a person, something was missing. There was no angst. Clearly some things would likely be missed in terms of what a youth would encounter. However there are some things that are encountered at any age that I felt needed to be discussed on some level.

When it came to Crisis Mode the mentality was to try and avoid making the subject matter gloomy. Generally going through things like: grief, depression, bullying, suicide, as well as betrayal are not easy. In life rain will fall. And things will not always go your way. But in the midst of that trust things will get better. You may sound like Job at times when going through rough times. However the important thing is not to give in despite how bad things are going.

There is no clear answer to why bad things happen at times. All you can do is endure and when possible take help when it is offered. There is no time table for any suffering you endure for a period of time. Grief is not something that goes away easily. Depending on how intense the loss is the grief will be all the more worse. Keeping the emotions bottled up is never a good thing. Pretending something did not happen does more harm than good as well.

You clearly want to put on a brave front and be strong for others. But if you are suffering a broken heart you need to heal that as soon as possible. Part of the recovery is trying to get out the worst of what you are feeling. Does that mean you will never feel bad somewhere down the line? Of course not, the pain will always be there. Learning to live with that pain will make what happens later on easier.

There are a number of resources out there to help you cope with what you are dealing with. But the only way they will be useful is if they address the problem directly that you are facing. So making an effort to tell people what is bothering you will a long way towards helping you move on from whatever went on before.

Along with seeking help do not forget the coping resources available through your faith. It is easy to forget God in what is going on. Along with what is happening do not forget to pray for help. There are passages in the bible that are encouraging and uplifting at times. A kind word goes a long way in cheering yourself up.

If you know someone that is going through a difficult situation do what you can to support them. As a friend or family member there are a number of things you could do to help and support that person. Sometimes the best thing to do is be a presence. When the person needs something they will likely tell you better what is needed. If you know what the situation is offer help but avoid smothering them.

Trust issues are bound to happen when you are betrayed by a friend. When someone burns you whether it was once or several times, it is not easy to openly trust people. Trying to figure who are really your friends and who are not is a difficult task. Then again explaining a force of nature is not always easy to do either. Trust is hard to gain and easy to lose. Some people can be taken at face value as honest and some cannot. The only thing to say is when you understand the type of person you are, the rest will fall into place somehow.

Bullying has not changed too much over the years. But the way it is done has taken on a new dimension especially with the internet. As a kid the main bullying I dealt with was possibly getting jumped playing in the park or bad treatment at school. It was mainly a local situation in the neighborhood if at all. However with the addition of the internet and social media, anything can be magnified. And people you probably will never meet in real life are now able to take nasty jabs at you verbally. Bad jokes and degrading comments hurt. And to say there is an easy solution to it would be a lie. But there are resources to help if you look. And like all things that come up if you know the problem a solution can be found.

I have had countless experiences with the situations mentioned in the chapter Crisis Mode. One area that I felt needed to be covered despite not having any personal experience in it was suicide. There are teens as well as adults that commit suicide for a number of reasons. To go into that completely would take more than what was said in that chapter. If you are feeling you are better off dead it is my sincere hope that you rethink that. Regardless of how bad things appear to be you never know if it will get better if you give up now. Just as Paul was there to prevent the jailor from killing himself, hopefully there is someone there to encourage you to take heart and know all is not lost.

Most important regardless of what is going on remember to take care of yourself. It is easy to get caught up in the various storms raging around you. Keep in mind to take care of your health especially in those situations. God rested and so should you. Get some rest. Make sure you eat something. Keep your health up as much as possible.

After all that is said what else could possibly be left to say right? Continuing what was said about health here are a few more things to say before closing out. You see biblical figures moving about working. And you probably feel if you are not working something is wrong.

Just note Moses moved about taking care of his people. But you did see points were he assigned things to others to avoid burning himself out. Humbling yourself and asking for help is not a bad thing. And during his encounters with God he was off somewhere quiet. So he did have moments of quiet in between the hustle of dealing with crowds.

Jesus is seen in the Gospels moving around preaching, teaching, among other forms of work. However he had moments where he withdrew from crowds to gather himself. Even after sending the disciples out on a mission, when they came back he took them somewhere quiet to gather themselves.

You need to do what you have to do for others. But make sure you take care of yourself in the process. Regularly eat something. And make sure you fuel your body the proper way. Get rest when you can. Work can be demanding at times but make sure you do not wear yourself out doing what you have to do. Balance priorities in terms of what needs to be done and what can be taken care of later on.

Not only take care of yourself physically, take care of yourself mentally as well. Feed your mind properly. Entertain yourself but also educate yourself as well. There is always something to learn. While educating yourself make sure you learn and understand what it means to be you, along with who the people around you are about. Most important make sure it is an honest look and not one based on stereotypes. Stereotypes can lead to ignorant ideas about groups of people as well as yourself. Searching for the true self in what you are about as well as others takes work. The better you understand who you are as a person as well as others the easier things will be in the long run.

After I was recruited as Verger, later on that month I was at the cathedral in conversation with a group of Vergers. They didn't know what to make of me at first because of my youthful appearance. But afterwards there was a sharing of advice. One bit of advice that stuck with me I will leave with you.

He told me to said pick my battles wisely. He said that with what I am involved in could lead to potential friction with others. That is because as Verger the ministry is a combination of other ministries so in aiding the church potential conflicts can happen. When you are involved in something at times you will have issues with what someone is doing. Or they may have issues with what you are doing. Regardless of the situation you are in, stick to your story if you have a strong case for it. Make sure you know who is on your side as well. If you have someone that clearly will back you in a situation do what you have to. Otherwise let it go and move on.

You are not perfect so allow yourself a moment to make mistakes. This does not mean you deliberately mess up doing something. You want to be successful and win. However if you treat everything you encounter as a learning experience you will learn either way. The most important thing is that you keep moving forward. There is always something new to learn.

Trends come and go. Some ideas are good ones that should be capitalized on. And some ideas should be left alone. Exercise honest judgment in a given situation when making a choice in what to do. You always have a choice both major and minor in what to do in a situation. You may have been involved in activities among other things because of other people but in the end you ultimately decide what you will do. The ball is in your court. Everything I said in this book is on a very basic level. What you do next is your choice. I wish you well on your journey. May it be rewarding and fulfilling. *"I have fought the good fight, I have finished the race, I have kept the faith"* (2 Tim. 4:7).

CHAPTER SEVEN

Message to the Parents

"And if a house is divided against itself, that house will not be able to stand" (Mk. 3:25).

For the record the previous chapter concluded the book. This chapter is a bonus. Shortly after taking over the Acolytes, I began doing Parent Meetings to get parents who barely knew me familiar with what I was doing. At the end of one of the meetings a father held a conversation with me addressing concerns about his son.

We spoke honestly to each other. The father clearly wanted his son to do well and it showed in his conversation. My response was that I would do everything possible to help while his son was here. But noted his son was around him more than he was me. So we would both need to work together in that regard.

It was this conversation that motivated the writing this chapter. This book discussed various topics aimed at helping your child in a number of areas. However there is only so much influence I can have. In order for things to get done it will take parental involvement to see it through. Children need positive role models as examples to grow as individuals. They also need parental involvement to help guide them. Parents will always be a factor in a child's life.

In an episode of the Cosby Show where Bill Cosby invited his son's school teacher to the house for a conversation. The son protested and said Bill should have gotten permission from him to invite the teacher. Bill then took a stack of bills out and gave it to his son asking whose names are on them. This was Bill's way of explaining to his son that this was his house so he makes the rules.

There is an interesting scene in the movie "Braveheart". It is around the funeral scene when a young William Wallace meets his uncle for the first time. After William's uncle says he will take raise and take care of him. They are next seen standing together with William seeming eager to hold a sword. That scene ends with the uncle saying to first learn how to use his head then he will learn how to use a sword. From that point in the movie we spring forward to when William has grown into an adult. As he becomes a leader there are on many occasions times William recalls lessons learned from his uncle. We do not know what family dynamic there was over the course of those years. But we can tell his uncle was a good mentor to him. Over the course of the movie when William Wallace was stuck he would reflect on what his uncle taught him and move on.

The examples from the Cosby Show and the movie Braveheart were used for a specific reason. In the case of the Cosby Show the example was the father exercising his authority. In the case of Braveheart you see someone stepping up to raise a child. Both cases show someone stepping up and taking responsibility for raising a child as well as exercising authority. A child will grow up one way or another. The outcome will depend on the circumstances, environment, and support surrounding the child.

Youth are the equivalent of Pawns on a Chessboard. Initially they are not that important or significant. However if you commit to the gradual progression of the Pawn's journey across the board to the end they become a more powerful player in the game. It may not be clear what is in store with the youth but if you commit to their gradual progression in life it's amazing what could happen.

There is not much discussion of childhood and family life in the bible. There are however calls to respect parents in both the Old and New Testaments. You see that in the Ten Commandments (Ex. 20:12; Deut. 5:16) as well as in numerous letters from Paul (Eph. 6:1-3; Col. 3:20). There is also a command to respect elders (Lev. 19:32). These situations need to be taught. Being respectful to adults is a learned habit.

The bible does not show family dynamics with a huge level of detail. The bible only shows glimpses that deal with certain situations. You would have to look elsewhere for the life and times of the people in the era you are reading. Just as the bible suggests how a child should respect parents and elders. It also gives hints on how a parent should raise a child (Eph. 6:4; Col. 3:21). There are two ways to say "that's my child". You can either say it with great delight or with great disgust. Here are some glimpses into family life from the bible.

We do not have details on daily family life concerning Jesus. Luke's Gospel has the most details of the childhood of Jesus. There is the famous telling of him as a child in the temple with his family looking for him. When they found him and were heading home this is what was said about him prior to meeting the adult Jesus *"Then he went down with them and came to Nazareth, and was obedient to them. His mother treasured all these things in her heart. And Jesus increased in wisdom and in years, and in divine and human favor"* (Lk. 2: 51, 52).

What does that say about the parenting skills of Mary and Joseph? Not too much. There is not a blueprint to follow from that reading. However later on in the Gospels it can be noted at certain times the text would say Jesus did something as was his custom. If he is doing something according to his custom it is likely he was raised to have certain habits. With that said his parents instilled in him habits which he carried into adulthood. Good habits start at home. Conditions vary however regardless of that. Balancing teaching along with discipline will go a long way in nurturing your child to grow into the individual you hoped they would become.

Do not be fixated with having things perfect for your child to grow. It is said that when Jesus was presented at the temple, Mary offered a pair of turtledoves or two young pigeons (Lk. 2:24). This falls in line with the rules established in Leviticus concerning the purification of women during childbirth (Lev. 12). The offering called for a lamb and a pigeon or turtledove (Lev. 12:6). If they could not afford sheep the alternative was two turtledoves or pigeons (Lev. 12:8). Since Mary offered turtledoves or pigeons it is likely that the family was poor since that was the alternative offering. This probably means Jesus grew up in humble conditions. Regardless of the conditions Jesus grew up to do what was needed to be done.

The ideal family may be a married couple. Those are not the only types of families. There are families where the parents are not together for a variety of reasons. Not to forget blended families. There are a number of families in the Old Testament that fit the description of blended families. For example the family of Abraham for starters, he had sons from Hagar and Sarah. He later on had a wife named Keturah. We do not know much about the dynamic between Ishmael the son of Hagar, and Isaac the son of Sarah. But we do get a glimpse into the relationship of Hagar and Sarah. Hagar was sent away sometime after the birth of Isaac (Gen. 21: 8-14). Following the death of Sarah, Abraham married Keturah and then he had children with her. Abraham took care of them as well (Gen. 25: 1-6). At Abraham's funeral it was Isaac along with Ishmael who would bury him (Gen. 25:9). Abraham provided for all his children. As a parent we can take cues about looking after children under any condition.

This is not the part where I define the role of parents by gender. The only specific roles are in childbirth. Both sides should share a part in teaching, nurturing and protecting the child. Aside from that the part of raising the child varies on the situation. The parents are either together or separated. If the child is raised in a single parent home that means there is a slim partnership in raising the child. So the stress of raising a child or children weighs more on the parent. However do not lose hope if you are in a single parent situation.

In situations involving divorce or separation things could get complicated at times. Estranged parent/child relationships at times can be difficult. It depends on the bonds of the parent and child. If they want a relationship it will take work on both sides. Also when going through a rough situation involving splitting up it can be a confusing time for both sides. Make sure if things are difficult in a relationship that it does not harm the child. Children know something is wrong do what you can to make sure they understand why because they will react even if they do not know what is going on.

If there is a split try to avoid pitting children's emotions between parents. Maintain having them be respectful to you. When my parents split it was not an easy situation. When they started seeing other people there was naturally confusion. There was also a needing of someone to help me understand and accept what was going on. When it comes to other relations my rationale was two things. The first is my parents deserve to be happy. And as long as the relationship they are in was not the cause of the split there is nothing wrong with it. Second as long as my parents want me around I will always be open to a relationship with them. This does not need to be said but naturally my parents love me. And no one is above my parents. There will always be respect in regards to the relationships they are in, but no one is above my biological parents. I had a conversation like this numerous times because a visiting priest or bishop who appreciates what I do in church would ask me about family life.

Relationships after a split can become complicated as well. Introducing a child to someone that is not a parent can be rough if not approached right. Help the child understand why someone is around. They will work with you if they understand better what is going on. *"Train children in the right way, and when old, they will not stray"* (Prov. 22:6).

Times and culture may have changed, as well as a way of living has changed over the centuries. But human nature still remains for the most part the same. I know for a fact the same way I was afraid to be beaten by my parents the children in general that I mentor in the Acolytes have that same fear as well. One time during Acolyte Practice there was a conversation with one of the members. They were acting out that morning and I asked if they do this in choir rehearsal earlier. They said no because I did not know their parents. One of the parents stopped by and asked how things were going. After saying they were good as long as they listen, the child looked scared at their parent. And the parent gave them a look. Following that there was never a problem during rehearsal time. Again that is the role of parental involvement. Parents and teachers/mentors working together will help a child grow better.

There are usually no formal 'rites of passage' situations to use in raising a child. However you can teach them how to grow in stages. There will always be a generation gap. Experiences may differ. But there is still something we can teach each other. As parents, teachers, youth leaders, mentors collectively we can lay a foundation for a child to grow with. *"Now, discipline always seems painful rather than pleasant at the time, but later it yields the peaceful fruit of righteousness to those who have been trained by it"* (Heb. 12:11).

At times like this it is easy to draw upon the directions Paul gave Titus. Before launching into a series of directions regarding how Titus was to teach groups of people. He gave the following instructions at the beginning of the second chapter: *"But as for you, teach what is consistent with sound doctrine"* (Titus 2:1). As we make an effort to educate our children about the differences between right and wrong. May we do it effectively and with honestly.

Communication is important. In order for your child to learn and grow the way you hope they will a fair amount of communication needs to be established. When Jesus discusses foundations in Luke 6:46-49, he lays out the differences between following directions and not following directions. He says when someone taking instruction is similar to a man building a house on solid ground. And because the house was well built nothing could damage it. But someone who does not listen to instruction is similar to a man who built their house on a weak foundation and the end result is the house was destroyed.

In establishing a foundation there is a need to help them setup priorities. School of course is a priority. Help them manage time so school work is done. If they are involved in activities such as sports, or volunteer service make sure they know how to manage time in dealing with that so it does not later on overwhelm them. Also remember God rested. Jesus moved about preaching, teaching, among other forms of work. However the Gospels record that even he withdrew to gather himself. So it is important to have time to yourself where you rest, recharge, and begin with a new and better focus.

As skills and talent develop find ways to help them utilize that. And not only encourage growth but teach them to keep their options open. There are numerous ways to unlock their potential. The only limitation is the imagination. *"Divide your means seven ways, or even eight, for you do not know what disaster may happen on earth"* (Eccl. 11:2). So help them keep their options open while pursuing a goal.

The second and third chapters dealt with skill building. The second chapter dealt with to a degree speaking skills. The third chapter dealt with evaluating what your skills are and then figuring out how to fix what is lacking. When you find out the set of skills available you can build a team to compensate for what is missing. While watching the playoffs it is always interesting to hear coaches talk about executing their game plan. And then hear the players talk about how supportive they are of each other.

Some of the boys in the Acolytes have goals of playing professional sports. That is not a bad goal. However being 'nice' in a sport does not guarantee success on the field. I always say do not look at the regular season games only. Look at the preseason games and see how many players you never heard of or will ever see play in the regular season come to training camps to try out for a team. For every LeBron James, Kobe Bryant, Carmelo Anthony, Michael Jordan, Magic Johnson, Larry Bird, Dr. J, and so on there are hundreds of players that were stars in their schools that had a dream of getting into the NBA or any sport for that matter only to miss out. Some may get as close to the minor league teams of that franchise or play overseas.

And let us not forget this is a business. If you do not perform you are gone. And if you fail to follow instructions by coaches or mesh well with your teammates, you will not last on the team either. There is a chance you might be traded, put on waivers, and due to collective bargaining agreements there is also free agency and salary cap situations. Knowing who to surround yourself with to be successful is a must. Skill and talent will only go so far. Injuries may occur and possibly affect skills. Being grounded with a solid foundation before going anywhere is a must because it is easy to get lost in the glitz and glamour of sports. *"for, while physical training is of some value, godliness is valuable in every way, holding promise for both the present life and the life to come"* (1 Tim. 4:8).

Again I stress communication. There are numerous images out there that can influence your child. You need to be able to help them become motivated by the right images and influences. In sorting out the images we can establish a core to grow with. *"The purposes in the human mind are like deep water, but the intelligent will draw them out"* (Prov. 20:5).

In sorting out images please note information is becoming more widespread every day. Unless you live like a hermit it is safe to say your child will find out details one way or another. You may not be around your child all the time. But you can give them a foundation where regardless of whatever they are involved in they will likely make the right decisions you hoped for.

In the chapter titled Influences a variety of things are discussed. In the beginning of the chapter a discussion of following God took place. The path to following God varies depending on the habits of the church you follow. That part of the chapter was not meant to interfere with another group's doctrine. The discussion like everything else in this book was on a basic level. The goal was to give the reader ideas on what to do, not dictate it. So the reader was given an idea on what to do.

Then the discussion fell on entertainment and its role in our lives. Television, music, movies play a part our lives. At some point I discuss videogames. There are differences in what videogames I played as a child and what children are playing now. One thing I can also say that is different is that there was not rating system when I first started playing videogames. But as the technology advanced things became more detailed. When games like Mortal Kombat, and Doom made their way to consoles there was a panic. This was because of the strong violent content.

The rating system was established and along with the rating, the content in the game was listed as well. The way a game is rated will always be open to debate. The system is as flawed as we are individually. However we should not count on any form of entertainment to take on sole responsibility in anything. We need to pay attention to content and if we do not agree with it simply avoid supporting it. And explain to your child why you do not agree with the content.

After the mess involving the Grand Theft Auto IV game things got interesting because they found sexual content in the game, I was in a few conversations with people about that. Personally I never played the game. But found the reaction to be a bit much. The game was rated M for Mature. An M rated videogame is the equivalent of an R rated movie. The content listed was: Blood and Gore, Intense Violence, Strong Language, Strong Sexual Content, and Use of Drugs. This is usually the typical listing for a Grand Theft Auto game. When they submitted the content that was meant to be played in the game that was the review they received. It was unfortunate that people were able to hack the game and play a sex game. But where was the outrage when people found out you could pick up hookers and have sex in the car? Even as the details came out more my stance was still the same, the reaction was to a game that was already labeled inappropriate for kids. Following that situation there were ads in videogame magazines that stressed that people should not just read the rating of games but also read the back of the boxes to know the content.

In one conversation with a relative they raised concern about content in videogames. I pulled out three videogames one rated E for Everyone, one rated T for Teen, and one rated M for Mature. First I showed them

"The Punisher" which was rated M for Mature. Showed them the front of the game box with the rating clearly displayed. Then showed the back of the box which showed the contents listed: Blood and Gore, Drug Reference, Intense Violence, Strong Language. Naturally since the Punisher uses guns violence would be a major part of the game. And given he fights criminals a lot of the content is self explanatory. Although the 'Special Kills' and 'Special Interrogations' might raise alarms for concern.

For the T for Teen rated game I pulled out Tekken 5. All games in the fighting series were rated T up to this point. The contents on the back listed were: Language, Sexual Themes, Use of Alcohol and Tobacco, and Violence. I was not surprised about violence or any language. However I was surprised about the Sexual Themes. The goal of the game is to win the tournament with your fighter. However one of the female fighters during her victory celebration sounds like she is making (ahem) happy noises. The alcohol and tobacco content is probably because some of the fighting environments featuring an audience watching on in an arena setting. Language was a minor part of the game. Along any dialog with the characters during the course of the game there may be some taunting or trash talking. However it is rare if at all to hear cursing.

For kicks I added a game rated E for Everyone. The game was EA Sports NHL 2002. The contents listed were: Violence and Comic Mischief. I understood the violence mainly because of the body checking and fighting. The Comic Mischief was a surprise though. Unlike most games you hear mainly 'he scores', or 'what a save'. In this case one of the announcers provides comic relief. The Play by Play Announcer would be the straight man calling the action. The Color Commentary would make some wacky comment aimed at humor. This would lead to interesting reactions between the play by play and color commentary guys. For example if a team is losing badly the Color Commentary would say 'they aren't even playing my worst hockey'. The Play by Play Announcer would then say 'that is bad'.

Getting back to Grand Theft Auto the sexual content that changed the game to an Adults Only rating was content that was able to be unlocked by hacking into it. The makers of the game instead of trying to pull out content they did not mean to have in the game decided to cover it up and hope no one could find it. I am not an expert in game programming but there were a number of articles in gaming magazines talking about problems making games for consoles like the PlayStation 2.

When the game "Tomb Raider: The Angel of Darkness" came out it was delayed for a lengthy period of time. Then rushed out around the time that the movie "Tomb Raider: The Cradle of Life" was coming to theaters. There were complaints about poor playing control and combat was terrible. When "Legacy of Kain: Soul Reaver 2" arrived there were a few programming glitches. In the first Soul Reaver, gamers were able to backtrack and explore areas with new abilities gained during the game. In Soul Reaver 2 glitches would freeze the game making you reset and play through to that point again. Also originally it was going to be released on the original PlayStation but was later moved to PlayStation 2. Programming can be tricky. And sometimes this leads to votes as to whether to keep or toss features out of games just to insure the game gets completed on time.

Nice story get to the point right? The conversation was about the ratings system on games and what should be done about it. The goal of showing the games was to explain that there wasn't anything wrong with the ratings system. It can be debated on how reliable the system is but then again there is no fail safe way of doing anything. There is only so much responsibility the entertainment industry should take in what they put out. If you do not agree with the content then avoid supporting it. All the warning labels listed saying its inappropriate is visible. Also go the extra mile and explain to your child why you disagree with the content presented in the game. They will listen. And this may lead to creative dialogue where you collectively come to an agreement on things.

It is not just videogames that need to be looked out for. Along with paying attention to rating and content in videogames, pay attention to the movies as well. Sometimes the PG-13 movies are more R rated than the R movies. Movies like "The Lord of the Rings" trilogy and "King Arthur" at times were right there with the violence of R rated movies like "The Last Samurai", "Gladiator", or even "Braveheart". However the violence in the PG-13 movies lacked the gore that was in the R rated movies. So you saw the sword fights. But you did not see people hacked to pieces.

Spike Lee made an interesting point in his commentary on the "Malcolm X" DVD. During the scene involving drugs he pointed out that you never see the actors directly using drugs. He shot it with a hint of drug using. That is how he was able to maintain a PG-13 rating. This is a major difference from Scarface where you see Al Pacino at some point diving into a pile of cocaine.

When Quentin Tarantino was being interviewed for his recent movie "Django Unchained", there was one interview that did not go too well. It has been famously called on the internet as the Tarantino rant. The movie was released sometime after the tragic shooting at the Sandy Hook Elementary school in Connecticut. At this time there was a concern about violence in movies.

At one point the interviewer asked Quentin if there was a direct relation between movie violence and real life. Quentin got defensive and protested the need to answer that question going so far as to say people can 'Google' him for his thoughts on that subject. For the record I do not care much for Tarantino films. They put me to sleep. The only thing keeping me from falling completely asleep is the occasional violent scenes. I may not agree with the movies he makes. But I agree that movies are not directly to blame for the violence. There were violent movies before Tarantino and there will be violent movies after him. Everyone does not go to the movies and turn around drawing guns to start shooting anyone. There is always a much deeper motivation for that.

It is a mistake to scapegoat movies as the problem for violent behavior. Violent movies have an influence on people but it should not take the sole blame as to why people do massive shootings. In the movie "Raw Deal" Arnold Schwarzenegger near the end of the movie decides he is going to knock the bad guys dead. And then proceeds to do a drive by shooting blasting "Satisfaction" in his car. Then he makes his way to a building to kill everyone else.

We also need to pay attention to the content on TV and radio. I am not at all comfortable watching a game or TV show and seeing numerous commercials for enhancements and medications for dysfunctions. This is not just late night television. This is sometimes prime time if not sooner. On the radio there seems to be a lot of innuendo in songs. It is not new to Rap music. There was booty music before. 2 Live Crew anyone? However the standard on what is suitable to be played at certain times on the radio whether it is music or commercials is questionable. And whatever is playable can also be accessed on the internet. And the majority of the mobile phones out there have internet access. So people can use their web browsers to find explicit songs and videos.

Rap is popular within the group I mentor so the main discussion in the book about music was based on rap. Rap used to have more variety to it where people did not sound the same. Now it is mainly what sells and makes money. So the majority of the music is not always suitable for children. And rappers take on a personality like actors some they are not always doing what is portrayed as real life. Like wrestlers it is a gimmick that gets attention. Aside from that they are normal people like us trying to live their lives.

It may be discouraging the amount of violence, language and other content is accessible lately. However with that said teaching your child to sort out right and wrong is a must. A form of entertainment should not be raising your child. Allow your child to be entertained, and educate them on right and appropriate behavior. With the addition of the internet and social media/networking it is easier to find information on various things.

Establish good communications with those who are involved in your child's life. The one thing I found consistently within the group of kids following me in the Acolytes is that they do not always tell their parents what is going on. And I also found out they do not have the conversations with their parents that was common between my parents and me. For example my parents would ask how my day was and vice versa. Conversations like that need to become regular again. Parents are probably busier than mine ever was, but simple conversations like that go a long way in bonding and keeping better track of your child without smothering them.

When I was growing up my parents had me involved in a variety of activities and over time after figuring out what I liked stuck to that. Those were the activities that remained part of my life. Aside from school I was in the Boy Scouts and later the Acolytes. The basics from these groups became the foundation for me as a person. Groups established for children's activities if approached right will be a rewarding experience. A child will go initially because of the parent. However if they develop a solid reason to go they will progress in the group.

A member in my group once said they were worried about making mistakes. This led them to always want to be in the background and less active. Strangely enough the Acolytes are fairly active during the worship service. My response was make mistakes now while there are people here to support you. When you are alone then it will be harder to recover from what happened.

Honestly no one is perfect. So worry less about mistakes and more about learning from them. Anyone in a given time will make a mistake. There were a few times in church where I made a mistake. However my mentality is not that I made a mistake but how many caught it. With that said if a mistake does happen I act like it was supposed to go that way.

In the documentary "Art of Rap", rapper WC is talking with Ice T. WC comments on how Ice T played off a mistake on stage. The record player skipped so Ice T turned to the crowd and acted like they said something to him. Ice T later on discussed how when he messes up performing he would act like the microphone cut off and there was a technical problem. That leads to the song being restarted.

During Acolyte Practice I mentioned a mistake that happened during a service at the cathedral during the Absalom Jones service. In the Episcopal Church, Absalom Jones is recognized as a former slave turned Priest. During the Offertory Procession the Head Verger was leading the Offertory Procession. While watching from a distance both the other assisting verger and I noticed along there was mistake during the procession. The Head Verger almost made the wrong turn while heading past the Altar. He was about to turn the wrong way but quickly corrected himself before he did it. Afterwards the Head Verger made it clear something did happen. He laughed it off and moved on.

A child wants to be the best they can be. If they make mistakes they think it is the end of the world. We need to encourage them to do what they can and be able to accept the good with the bad. Allow them to have a competitive spirit that drives them to do well. But have a calming influence surrounding them when things do not go well or as planned. The fear of failure will always be there. We need to be there to help dust them off when failure occurs and say keep at it, and assure them things will be ok. Enjoy the journey and appreciate the learning experience that happens on it. The journey sometimes is more of a story than the outcome. This book is about growth. With that said if a new skill was attained during the journey that is a good thing.

The hardest chapter for me to write for this book was Crisis Mode. This is supposed to be an inspirational book for the youth. However since my intentions were to cover possible areas a child let alone a person would go through aside from interactions with others, this chapter I felt was necessary. Bad things that cause strife can happen at any age whether it is random struggles to personal tragedy to bad treatment from others.

Like everything else discussed the goal was to keep it basic so hopefully the topics did not come off too gloomy in that chapter.

Writing that chapter was draining both mentally and emotionally at times. But on a personal level felt necessary to be included in the book. Dealing with grief, depression, and other types of emotional strife can at times be challenging. Just remember as adults we can easily get help for our needs. Youth are minors so they need parental consent and adult supervision in getting help. So there is a need to not just be there for your child. You need to have a comfortable level of communication with them to where they feel able to come to you on a variety of topics that bother them.

It took awhile before I was able to openly talk to my parents about certain issues that bothered me. There was always a level of trust with them. Eventually feeling comfortable talking about situations that bothered me and believing that they would not judge me took some time. Afterwards things were comfortable enough to speak freely without being offensive of course and get things off my chest in an honest way.

I covered a variety of topics within the chapters of this book. However one topic that was not discussed in much detail was personal relationships. Friendships and working relationships were discussed to a degree. But talking about loving relationships was not discussed in any way here. At times members of the Acolytes ask me for advice a variety of topics. One topic I try to not speak too much on is relationships. My personal feeling is that it should be more the parent's role to discuss that. *"And I will take you for my wife forever; I will take you for my wife in righteousness and in justice, in steadfast love, and in mercy. I will take you for my wife in faithfulness; and you shall know the LORD"* (Hos. 2:19, 20).

Being in love takes on a whole host of emotions and situations for anyone, so talking about relationships need to be handled with care. Teaching responsible and healthy habits will go a long way in terms of how your child deals with their personal life. Encourage them to follow their heart and help them overcome heartbreak. Just as I said earlier that they should not be afraid to make mistakes, encourage them not to feel disappointed in any possible rejection that may come. Keep at it and encourage them to pursue relationships and be involved in healthy ones that help them grow. All we can do is plant the seed and help prepare them for what may come. The outcome is ultimately up to them. So while we prepare and teach an important thing we must stress is encouraging responsible behavior. Let them enjoy their life and have fun. Along the way make sure they know how to avoid things that will get them in trouble and cause regret. I leave that to you.

When my mentor suggested I write a book for the youth there were plenty of reservations on my part. After really sitting down and thinking about it, that is when ideas for topics formed to talk about. When they were better fleshed out then it felt better moving forward in doing this. My goal was not to write a book simply for your child to read and possibly learn from. The goal was to write a book where they may learn something and that the parent can read and maybe have a conversation with them.

In writing the topics the idea was not to dumb it down for children and youth. They see and understand a number of things. But they are not fans of lengthy lectures. With that said the approach while writing was to get to the point as soon as possible without a lengthy speech. In closing it is my sincere hope that this book found an audience that enjoyed what they read, and that there was something useful for them as well. *"Discipline your children while there is still hope; do not set your heart on their destruction"* (Prov. 19:18).